THE LANG
THOMAS

Raymond Chapman

DATE DU

M
MACMILLAN

THE LANGUAGE OF LITERATURE
General Editor: N. F. Blake

Published titles
The Language of Shakespeare N. F. Blake
The Language of Chaucer David Burnley
The Language of Wordsworth and Coleridge Frances Austin
The Language of Irish Literature Loreto Todd
The Language of D. H. Lawrence Allan Ingram
The Language of Thomas Hardy Raymond Chapman

Further titles are in preparation.

THE LANGUAGE OF LITERATURE
General Editor: N. F. Blake

First published 1990

Published by
MACMILLAN EDUCATION LTD
Houndmills, Basingstoke, Hampshire RG21 2XS
and London
Companies and representatives
throughout the world

British Library Cataloguing in Publication Data
Chapman, Raymond, 1924-
  The language of Thomas Hardy.– (Language of
  Literature).
  1. Fiction in English. Hardy, Thomas, 1840– 1928–
  Critical studies
  I. Title II. Series
  823′.8

ISBN 0-333-47160-1
ISBN 0-333-47161-X Pbk

Contents

Note on Texts

Hardy revised his work a great deal, particularly between the periodical and volume publication of some of the novels. Unless a variant is specifically noted, all quotations from his novels are taken from the New Wessex paperback edition, published by Macmillan, London (1974, reissued 1985). The following abbreviations are used for references in parentheses after quotations, followed by the page number.

AL	*A Laodicean* 1881
DR	*Desperate Remedies* 1871
FFM	*Far from the Madding Crowd* 1874
HE	*The Hand of Ethelberta* 1876
JO	*Jude the Obscure* 1896
MC	*The Mayor of Casterbridge* 1886
PBE	*A Pair of Blue Eyes* 1873
RN	*The Return of the Native* 1878
TD	*Tess of the D'Urbervilles* 1891
TM	*The Trumpet Major* 1880
TT	*Two on a Tower* 1882
UG	*Under the Greenwood Tree* 1872
W	*The Woodlanders* 1887
WB	*The Well-Beloved* 1897
D	*The Dynasts* 1904–8 followed by part, act and scene.

Poems are cited as *P*, followed by page number in *Thomas Hardy: the Complete Poems*, edited by James Gibson (Macmillan, London, 1976, reprinted 1983).

Other sources frequently quoted are:

CL	*The Collected Letters of Thomas Hardy*, edited by R.L. Purdy and M. Millgate (Clarendon Press, Oxford, 7 volumes, 1982–8).
PW	*Thomas Hardy's Personal Writings*, edited by Harold Orel (Macmillan, London, 1967).

EL   *The Early Life of Thomas Hardy 1840–1891* by Florence Emily Hardy (Macmillan, London, 1928).

LY   *The Later Years of Thomas Hardy 1892–1928* by Florence Emily Hardy (Macmillan, London, 1930).

1 Thomas Hardy: Life and Work

If Thomas Hardy could have chosen the period of history during which to live his long life, he could hardly have found one which would see greater changes in every aspect of British society. He was born three years after Victoria became Queen and died ten years after the end of the Great War. Melbourne was Prime Minister when he was born, Baldwin when he died. He was born when Dickens was beginning to make a name with his early novels and before the Brontë sisters, George Eliot or Trollope had published. When he died the leading writers in English were Virginia Woolf, T. S. Eliot, E. M. Forster and James Joyce. Shaw and Wilde, who brought the English theatre back to a degree of literary and intellectual quality, were born when he was in his adolescence. He was born when few men, and no women, had a parliamentary vote; he died in the year in which women eventually got the vote on full equality with men. He saw the railways spread all over the British Isles, followed by the motor car and then the aeroplane. He lived through the intellectual revolutions created in their respective spheres by Darwin, Marx and Freud.

It is not surprising to find in what he wrote a strong nostalgia for the past, a sense of both personal and national history which extends to find kinship even with the vanished worlds of Saxon, Roman and prehistoric humanity. He regretted many of the changes through which he lived, particularly the disappearance of the rural way of life which had continued almost unbroken for centuries in his native county. Yet he was also a true Victorian in accepting new developments and acknowledging that in some ways conditions of life were better. Although he cared deeply for the past, he never minimised its discomforts and cruelties, never

1

looked for the golden age which many contemporaries found in favoured periods of history. He could feel oppressed by the 'ache of modernism' which afflicts his own Tess, but he could also recognise and partly welcome the challenge of a new age.

He was born on 12 June 1840 in the hamlet of Higher Bockhampton in Dorset, three miles from the county town of Dorchester. His father, also named Thomas, was in a small way of business as a mason and builder, an employer of other men and thus raised socially a little above the labourers who worked for wages. The family was poor enough, but Hardy grew up with the sense of hierarchy which was strong in the rural community. The distinction between the 'workfolk' and those who had any kind of property or trade of their own would often have been scarcely visible to an observer from the outside world, but it was real enough for those whom it concerned and was to play its part in the relationships in Hardy's novels. His mother was more conscious of status than his father and was anxious that her son should do well in life. There is a recollection of her with Mrs Dewy in *Under the Greenwood Tree*, who objects to her husband saying 'taties' for potatoes, 'in such a work-folk way'. Thomas was the first child, to be followed by a brother and two sisters.

When he was eight, Hardy was sent to the National School which had been built at Bockhampton with money from Mrs Julia Martin. Purchase of the Kingston Maurward estate in 1844 had made the Martin family the principal landowner in the cluster of hamlets which Hardy later called 'Mellstock'. Young Thomas was a favourite of the childless Mrs Martin, who admitted him to the great house and showed him much affection. The relationship had a lasting effect on him and he retained a somewhat romantic feeling for her over many years. Love which is checked by difference of birth and wealth, usually the love of a man for a woman socially above him, is a theme in several of his novels. Mrs Martin's approval ended abruptly when his parents sent him to the British School in Dorchester. It was a reasonable move for a boy showing capacity for more than a village school could provide, but it offended the Martins and led to the elder Thomas Hardy losing the estate business.

For the next eight years Hardy took the daily walk into Dorchester. When the headmaster, Isaac Last, set up a more advanced school of his own in 1853, Hardy transferred to it. While his formal education was being thus developed, his mind was being formed in many other ways. The family attended regularly the little church at Stinsford, where he became familiar with the Bible and the Book of Common Prayer, which are often quoted or echoed in his writing. In later years the country church became an image of the stability and tradition which were already disappearing, and he put his love for it into many fictional scenes and into poems like 'Afternoon Service at Mellstock' and 'A Church Romance'. The latter poem commemorates the first love of his parents, when his father played the fiddle in the church band before the coming of an organ. Musical talent was inherited by the son, who sometimes played the fiddle for country dances and came to know the old secular tunes as well as the psalm settings. The recreations of dances, harvest suppers and parties to celebrate family events kept up a tradition of many centuries. The young Hardy watched it all, listened to the stories around the fire on winter evenings, and came to know intimately the notable characters of the community.

On leaving school in 1856, he was articled to John Hicks, a Dorchester architect. The study and practice of architecture was to occupy him for many years; his novels and poetry would have much to say of church design and restoration. Architects and stonemasons appear among his characters, together with the older country craftsmen that he knew so well. His work with Hicks brought him into contact with young men of his own age, including the son of the local Baptist Minister, with whom he argued about deep theological matters like baptismal regeneration. He was also befriended by an older man, Horace Moule, one of the sons of the vicar of Fordington on the outskirts of Dorchester. The elder Moule was well known locally as a campaigner for sanitary reform, a champion of the poor and a hero in the cholera epidemic of 1854. His son, Horace, took an interest in Hardy, helped him in his study, advised him on reading and raised his aspirations above the limits of a small country town. Hardy began to dream of a university education and perhaps the status of holy orders. At about this time he wrote some of his first poems; it was a love which continued long after he eventually abandoned fiction. Sadly, Moule did better for his young friend than for himself. He was unable to settle to a career, began to drink heavily, and in 1873 he took his own life. The news was a deep shock to Hardy, with a sadness which remained.

Hardy's decision to leave Dorchester in 1862 seems to have been taken quickly and for no clear reason. It has been suggested that there was an unhappy love affair with an older woman employed in one of the local shops. Whatever the motive, Hardy went to London, armed only with two letters of introduction. It was a big decision for a young man who, like most of his class at that time, had seldom moved more than a few miles away from his home. However, London did not devour him as it did so many country folk in both the fiction and the reality of the period. He found a place in the office of Arthur Blomfield, son of a former Bishop of London, a leading architect who was particularly concerned with the restoration of old churches and the building of new ones in the Gothic style. Hardy showed promise in his profession; he won competitive prizes, he executed commissions for Blomfield and was entrusted with a little original work.

Like all young men then and later, he found more in life than work. Despite the restriction of a meagre salary and lodgings some distance from the centre, he made the most of London. The capital was changing rapidly in those years, notably in the expansion of public transport, which both followed and hastened its growth into the suburbs. From Blomfield's new office in Adelphi Terrace, Hardy could see Charing Cross station being built. The new underground railway made it easier to move between lodgings, work and pleasure. Hardy exchanged rural life for metropolitan, Stinsford church for St Stephen's, Westbourne Park, country dances in the barn for dancing at Willis's Rooms. He went to the theatre, the opera, and especially to art galleries. He began to keep a notebook on painters and paintings; his gift of visual observation, begun in the countryside and trained in architecture, now developed into a love of art. Yet though he found so much to interest him in London, and returned many times in later years, it was never home for him. His major novels are set almost entirely in Wessex. The London scenes which he wrote seldom contain his best work: there is a sense of unreality in the life and the people. London gave him much in the formative years of his early manhood, but it did not win him away from the past.

In 1867 he returned to work with Hicks in Dorchester. Now he was often sent out to deal with the restoration of country churches, a labour which he regretted later when 'restoration' came to seem an interference with natural development and often a destruction of living tradition. He is scathing about such work in several novels, particularly *Jude the Obscure*, and in poems like 'The Levelled Churchyard'. Yet, as a writer, he gained much from those years, as he added to his knowledge of Dorset and the neighbouring counties. The area which would become 'Wessex' was growing familiar to him, and his stock of country lore and characters was increasing.

He was at work in another way as well. In 1868 he submitted to the publishing firm of Macmillan a novel called *The Poor Man and the Lady*. It was read by John Morley, who found promise but advised against publication. There was a similar response from George Meredith, reading for Chapman and Hall. Meredith, already famous as a novelist, met Hardy and advised him to try again 'with a stronger plot and an artistic rather than a social purpose'. Hardy then offered the manuscript to Tinsley, who offered to publish it at the author's expense – an offer which Hardy wisely, though probably rather from lack of money, refused. He used sections of the manuscript in later books, and published part of it in 1878 as a novella entitled *An Indiscretion in the Life of an Heiress*. Set largely in London, this tells of how a country schoolmaster tries to break into fashionable society for the love of a rich young woman. It develops one of Hardy's favourite themes but is not greatly successful in either character or setting and suggests that Morley and Meredith judged the original book rightly. Hardy was to have many more disagreements with critics. The inauspicious start was lost in later success, but he never ceased to be sensitive to the opinions of reviewers.

He was now working for Hicks on a more casual basis, while he took time for writing. When Hicks died in 1869, Hardy accepted an offer of architectural work from Crickmay in Weymouth. In 1870 he was given an assignment which extended the borders of his fictional Wessex and changed his personal life. Crickmay sent him to St Juliot in Cornwall, to advise on the restoration of the village church. There he met the sister-in-law of the Rector, Emma Lavinia Gifford, a meeting which he described in the ecstatic poem 'When I set out for Lyonnesse'. He came back to Dorset convinced that he had met his ideal. It was not the first of his attachments; he was always easily attracted by women and would often make up a romantic fantasy about a pretty girl seen in passing or encountered for a moment. In London he had been fond of a girl called Eliza Nicholls, and later of her sister, Jane. Back in Dorchester he seems to have been drawn to thoughts of marriage with his cousin Tryphena Sparks. This affair came to nothing, and there may be a memory of it in the comments on the marriage of cousins in *Jude the Obscure*.

Hardy was accepted by Emma Gifford and began one of those long engagements common in the Victorian age. Meanwhile he continued his attempts to become a novelist. In 1871 *Desperate Remedies* was published by Tinsley, with a subsidy from the author. It shows the effect of Meredith's advice that he should create a 'stronger plot'. A melodramatic story, with a heavy villain, scandalous secrets and a spectacular fire, it is an attempt on the sensational novel which Reade and Collins had made popular. Too dependent on a tortuous plot and a number of stock characters, it is yet given distinction by the heroine, Cytherea Graye, who maintains her interest throughout the book and is the first of Hardy's memorable women. There are some fine dramatic scenes and the pleasure of rustic characters who comment on the action, but it is more valuable as the pioneer of Hardy's greatness than in its own right.

A year later *Under the Greenwood Tree* was published, the copyright being sold to Tinsley for thirty pounds. It was Hardy's first true presentation of his region of Wessex, based largely on his native Dorset but extending as far north as Berkshire and as far west as Cornwall. Although much was still to be developed, the new novel showed where his best work would lie. Set in the area of his childhood, with his parents and acquaintances as originals for some of the characters, it evokes a world which was already passing away. Alone among Hardy's novels, it is an entirely happy story, with only the temporary clouding of problems in young love, and ending, like many Victorian novels, with a suitable marriage. For the modern reader its delight is largely in the sayings of the country people and the response of the village choir dispossessed by a new organ. While some have criticised Hardy's class-sense and rural snobbery in his portrayal of the 'workfolk', most readers are content with the delight of the story, the vivid descriptions of natural and domestic scenes and the rendering of speech in the Dorset dialect. All these things became characteristic of Hardy's later and more profound fiction.

In 1873 a new novel began serial publication in the *Cornhill Magazine*. With *Far from the Madding Crowd* Hardy showed himself to be a writer of importance. He brings into the peaceful Dorset setting a story of unhappy marriage, betrayal and violent death, ending in calm and reconciliation. In Bathsheba Everdene he created a type that recurs in later books: a woman of some standing in her neighbourhood, efficient and decisive in managing the business side of her life but easily swayed in her emotions. Bathsheba makes two mistaken choices before settling down with the shepherd Gabriel Oak who has loved her through all her troubles. The fate of Fanny Robin, dying in the workhouse with her illegitimate child, reflects the stories of humble sorrows which Hardy had often heard. Sergeant Troy, who forsakes Fanny and proves a bad husband to Bathsheba, rises above the villain of melodrama but lacks the subtlety of Hardy's later creations. The workfolk again provide a commentary on the action, and give a sense of peace and country routine to counterpoint the tragic main plot.

Although the critics were not universally favourable, *Far from the Madding Crowd* brought Hardy much praise and gave him status as a novelist. The serial publication had another consequence. The editor of the *Cornhill*, Thackeray's successor in the post, was Leslie Stephen who was later the father of Virginia Woolf. Stephen liked his new contributor and a friendship grew up which did something to fill the gap left by the death of Moule. Stephen helped to widen Hardy's reading, and also acted as a catalyst in the movement away from the simple faith of his early years. Hardy was attending church less often, and was feeling less satisfied with orthodox Christian dogma. When Stephen renounced the holy orders which he had taken many years before, he asked Hardy to witness the formal document.

The development of Hardy's religious position was never uncomplicated. Chesterton's description of him as the 'village atheist' was grossly unfair, and he himself in old age denied the name and described himself as an agnostic. He certainly kept a strong attachment to the Church of England as a link with tradition and as the vehicle of the public worship which he loved. He continued to attend church services from time to time throughout his life, and seldom missed the chance of a cathedral evensong. He was prepared after many years to describe himself as a believing and practising member of the Church of England, and he stood as godfather for a baptism as late as 1922. He never ceased to care about the spiritual dimension of life, but he could find no easy comfort in orthodox belief and was sometimes sharply critical of those who did. Perhaps, like his own Jude Fawley, 'he might go on believing as before, but he professed nothing'. If he had remained totally convinced, or had become militantly atheist, his work might have been less profound than it is.

While his spiritual doubts were as yet kept to himself, personal experience played a large part in *A Pair of Blue Eyes*, published in 1873. The story of his visit to St Juliot and his love for Emma lies beneath the tale of the young architect, Stephen Smith, who goes on a similar errand. Stephen and Elfride, here made the rector's daughter, have a course of troubled love which comes to a sad conclusion. Elfride proves to be what the Victorians called a flirt, and becomes involved with Stephen's older friend, Henry Knight – based partly on Horace Moule. In the end she marries neither of them, but the young Lord Luxellian. After some years, Stephen and Knight travel back to Cornwall together, in the train which is carrying Elfride's coffin. It is not one of Hardy's great novels, too personal to make a deep human statement but too concealed and inconclusive to be a successful autobiographical novel. It probably helped to release some of Hardy's own tensions and to free him for better things. Other writers have done as much and more with their own stories. Some, like Dickens, Lawrence and Joyce, have also created great novels in so doing.

Despite the forebodings which this novel might have suggested, the engagement ended with marriage in 1874. Hardy took his bride to France for the honeymoon; it was perhaps characteristic rather than suitable that he included a visit to the Paris morgue. Emma was not entirely happy with foreign ways and was quite thankful to return and start making a home at Surbiton on the Surrey side of London. Hardy was now confident enough of his success as a writer to have given up architecture and devoted himself to writing. In the following year he published *The Hand of Ethelberta*, a story which moves between Dorset and London following the fortunes of a young widow who gains fame as a professional storyteller. Her deception to conceal her humble origin is complicated by her father and brother being employed in London. The tearing of Dorset men from the Dorset scene never worked very well for Hardy. We tend to lose patience with Ethelberta as she weighs up her London suitors and eventually marries a rich old lord. Her crises of conscience are not very convincing, and the marriage of her former admirer to her unsophisticated sister seems patched. There are some good moments, like the dinner party where Ethelberta is a guest and her father the butler, and her discovery that the fashionable suitor, Neigh, is really a horse-knacker. The novel as a whole leaves most readers neither uplifted nor greatly entertained.

Hardy and Emma did not stay very long in London. They returned to Dorset, first to Swanage and then to the little town of Sturminster Newton. Here Hardy worked at the first of his really great novels, which appeared in volume form in 1878 after serialisation in both a British and an American magazine. After *The Return of the Native*, no one could doubt that here was a major writer of fiction. The world of Egdon Heath is at once wholly local and yet a stage for human drama not limited by space or time. The 'rustic chorus' of workfolk provides a continuity of normal life accompanying the tortured central action. Eustacia marries Clym Yeobright in the false glamour of his having returned from Paris, deserts him when he becomes almost blind and is drowned when running away with her new lover, Damon Wildeve. The marriage of Wildeve's widow to her faithful suitor, Diggory Venn, the itinerant reddleman who travels selling colouring for marking sheep, ends the book on a peaceful note. Clym, whom Hardy once described as 'the nicest of my heroes', finds his vocation as a sort of humanist preacher. The conclusion may be tame, but what we remember about the book is vivid and tragic – the conflicts of character in the impersonal loneliness of the heath, with a sense of human weakness and nobility mingled in people whose fate can move us though their way of life is remote.

Hardy produced nothing so fine over the next few years but he continued to establish his position as a novelist and to do work which is far from negligible. In 1878 he and Emma moved back to London and took a house in Tooting. His fame was spreading and he came back not as an architect's assistant but as a distinguished man of letters. He joined the Savile Club and was a luminary in the literary world. Dickens and Thackeray were dead; George Eliot died in 1880 and Trollope in 1882. For the rest of the century only

Meredith could claim comparable status, and time has treated him less well than Hardy.

His next novel, *The Trumpet Major*, appeared in 1880. It is unique among his full-length stories in being set in a period much earlier than his own. He had always been fascinated by the time of the Napoleonic Wars, and liked to claim kinship with the Thomas Hardy who had been Nelson's flag-captain and later an admiral. Memories of the time lingered into his own childhood; the poem 'One We Knew' recalls how his grandmother heard the news of the execution of Louis XVI. Captain Hardy makes a brief appearance in the novel, but the main plot revolves around the love for one woman of two brothers, one a sailor and the other a trumpet major. It is a gentle book, with no villain more fierce than the boastful and cowardly Festus Derriman who tries to win Anne Garland from the brothers. There is much humour, notably from the brothers' father, Miller Loveday, and the country people for whom Napoleon is as feared and as remote as the devil. There are no early deaths, no serious violence, no disastrous marriages, and the darkness falls only in prospect as John Loveday goes 'to blow his trumpet until silenced for ever upon one of the bloody battle-fields of Spain'.

London never served Hardy well for long. He fell ill at Tooting and *A Laodicean* was largely dictated from his bed. By the time it appeared Hardy and Emma were back in Dorset living at Wimborne Minster. This novel tells of another of Hardy's influential but indecisive women. Paula Power is enabled by her father's industrial wealth to buy the ancient Stancy castle and establish herself as a lady of quality. She is the Laodicean – lukewarm in faith and in love; the book begins with her refusing the adult baptism to which she had committed herself, the Baptist minister being reminiscent of the father of Hardy's friend in Hicks's office. It ends with her acceptance of George Somerset, the impoverished young architect who came to redesign her castle and fell in love with her. In the meantime, others have schemed to secure her wealth through marriage and been thwarted. It is a story of an architect's successful suit in an ambience more exalted than that of St Juliot.

The love of the poor man and the lady appears again with *Two on a Tower* in 1882. The poor lover is now a village boy who has become an astronomer and is allowed to use a tower in the squire's estate for his observations. In the absence of the squire, his unhappy wife Viviette falls in love with Swithin the astronomer and marries him after a false report of her husband's death abroad. When the husband really is dead and Swithin returns to claim his wife, she dies suddenly in his arms. It is all rather unconvincing, but the real Hardy comes through with Swithin's old grandmother, and the satirical portrayal of the Bishop of Melchester who woos and for a time is married to Viviette. The irony of Swithin's first sight of his wife after several years, when he realises how much older she is, may possibly be a recollection of Hardy's meeting in adult life with Julia Martin.

Hardy moved to Dorchester in 1883 and lived near the centre of the town while a house was being built for him on the outskirts. He personally designed and supervised his new home and called it Max Gate, a more elegant rendering of Mack's Gate after the keeper of a tollgate formerly on the spot. Hardy and Emma moved into the house in 1885 and remained there until their deaths. Their lives moved on with few outward events; Dorset was their home but there were frequent stays in London where Hardy was now an honoured guest at fashionable houses. He met most of the leading literary figures of the day and in time received honorary degrees and, an honour precious to him, the freedom of Dorchester. There were several visits to the Continent, but Hardy never travelled a great distance and, unlike many Victorian men of letters, did not go to America.

Although few ripples showed on the surface, all was not calm in the depths of the marriage. Emma was strict and had developed a strong Evangelical faith which was affronted by Hardy's growing scepticism. She herself had aspirations to authorship and tended to be jealous of his success. She had written but not published a novel which gave Hardy ideas for some scenes in his own work. In *A Pair of Blue Eyes*, Elfride produces a short novel which is unfavourably reviewed by Henry Knight. Emma did, however, give a great deal of time and care to helping her husband and copying his manuscripts. Their brief courtship and the long engagement with infrequent meetings had not given them time to know one another properly, and Hardy the successful author had changed in many ways from the young architect's assistant. The marriage was childless; they remained loyal, but ill at ease.

Art is often created out of tension. Hardy was entering

upon his greatest period as a novelist. The years of residence in Dorchester helped him to portray its fictional counterpart with *The Mayor of Casterbridge* in 1886. Here he tells the life of Michael Henchard, who sells his wife to a sailor in a drunken fit, lives to repent, grows rich and becomes mayor of the county town. His fortunes start to decline after he has taken Farfrae, a young Scot, into his business, and his wife has returned. After the wife's death, Henchard learns that his supposed daughter is really the sailor's child. Farfrae prospers and takes over the business, after marrying a woman for whom Henchard has once had an attachment. Henchard dies alone and penniless; Farfrae's wife dies and he marries Henchard's stepdaughter. The story is in itself a simple recital of misjudgement and commercial ill luck among ordinary people, but Hardy elevates it to a height of tragedy and creates in Michael Henchard one of the greatest characters in fiction. It is by any standard a major novel and would in itself justify Hardy's reputation.

Although *The Woodlanders*, published in 1887, must be accounted among Hardy's great novels, it has never had the popularity of the others. Set in a deeply forested area of Dorset, it seems to fall under the shadow of the trees and not rise to the full heights of pity and terror of which Hardy was capable. Yet it has power of its own in a tale of unhappy marriage and hopeless love, as Marty South pines for Giles Winterbourne, who in turn desires Grace Melbury – each aspiring a little higher in social class. Grace marries the local doctor, a newcomer who is unfaithful to her with a rich widow. The theme of unequal social matching is strong, and Grace's unhappiness allowed Hardy to write about recent changes in the divorce law and new possibilities of freedom. The killing of the widow is sheer melodrama and would have fitted better into *Desperate Remedies*. But the scenes of country life, of tree-planting and cider-making, show Hardy at his best, and the death of Giles, with Marty's elegy, is as moving as anything he wrote: 'No, no, my love, I never can forget 'ee; for you was a good man, and did good things'.

During these years, Hardy was also writing short stories; *Wessex Tales* came out as a volume in 1888. His greatest work in fiction was yet to come. In 1891 he published *Tess of the D'Urbervilles*, probably the best known of his novels. Generations of readers have been moved by the story of how Tess is seduced by a rich young man, left with an illegitimate child who dies, and eventually deserted by her high-principled husband, Angel Clare, when he learns her secret. The execution of Tess for the killing of her seducer after she has gone back to him, ends the book on the darkest note that Hardy had yet touched. It is a tale of sorrow upon sorrow, of a girl doomed to misery in the indifferent world which she sees as a 'blighted star'. But there is also the rich life of the countryside in its different moods and tasks. The scenes in the dairy where Tess meets Angel and is happy for a time, combine the pastoral idyll with realism. The contemporary reception of the book was, predictably, mixed. Many readers and reviewers were affronted by the open presentation of seduction and illegitimacy, and Hardy's grim comment at the end, 'the President of the Immortals, in Aeschylean phrase, had ended his sport with Tess'. The sub-title, 'A Pure Woman', did nothing to appease them.

The death of Hardy's father in 1892 broke another link with the past and perhaps made him more dissatisfied with his domestic state. His next novel had much to say of marital unhappiness. While the earlier novels have their light and even joyful episodes, there is little relief in *Jude the Obscure*, published in 1896. Hardy put something of himself into the central character, reaching out to the darker side of his life and ignoring the better. Jude Fawley shares Hardy's early thoughts of going to a university and becoming a clergyman. A disastrous early marriage hampers him, and his arrival at Christminster (Oxford) brings only frustration as he finds the college doors closed to a working man. The theme of divorce now becomes important; Jude frees himself from his wife, and his cousin Sue is divorced by her husband, a schoolmaster older than herself. Jude and Sue live together and have children but always fear to take the decisive step of marriage. Eventually they go back to their spouses after the terrible death of their children. Jude dies, alone and neglected, in the university city that he had vainly sought to enter. The end is unrelievedly stark; even in *Tess of the D'Urbervilles* there is a gleam of light in the pairing of Angel and Tess's sister, but here there is only vanity and broken hopes.

Some admirers of Hardy dislike *Jude the Obscure*: others find it perhaps his greatest novel, strangely uplifting in its confrontation of human misery. As Hardy wrote in the poem 'In Tenebris', and later quoted in his justification: 'If a way to the Better there be, it exacts a full look at the Worst.' The critics of the time were almost unanimous in their condemnation. Hardy had offended not only by the overt portrayal of scepticism, as Jude moves from deep devotion to loss of orthodox faith and Sue follows the reverse course. He had also been too frank in his account of sexual frustration and revulsion, and he had struck at the ideal of marriage and the family. The Victorian age which was coming to an end, and whose demise he had partly depicted, struck back at him. One critic headed his review 'Jude the Obscene' and another described the book as 'the strongest illustration of what Art can come to when given over to exposition of the unclean'.

It has often been said that Hardy abandoned fiction because of the hostile reception of *Jude the Obscure*. Certainly he had always been sensitive to criticism, and the attacks on this book distressed him considerably. Yet the matter is probably not so simple; bad reviews may have hastened rather than determined his choice. Poetry had always been his first love and he regarded it as the more serious literary genre. He had now made a bold statement in fiction of his attitude and it was difficult to see what could follow. Nor was it easy for a man of nearly sixty to accommodate the many changes in society as the twentieth century approached. He may have felt, as E. M. Forster felt about the world after 1918, that he could no longer put it into fiction.

For whatever reason, he wrote no more novels. The last to be published was *The Well-Beloved* in 1897, but this had been written earlier. It is a curious book, the story of a man who seeks for his ideal in love and finds it after in three generations of women from his native locality. A story of personal frustration combined with worldly success, it may again be an image of Hardy's life as he saw it. The setting moves between London and the Isle of Portland, an area of Wessex that had not been closely used in earlier work. There are comparatively few characters and even the protagonist, Jocelyn Pierston, who vainly pursues happiness for forty years, does not fully come to life.

Hardy's main work for the remaining thirty years of his life was in poetry. His collected poems number over nine hundred. It is often difficult to place them chronologically; some go back to his early years, but most were written in the twentieth century. Hardy is essentially a modern poet, although he was influenced by the ballad tradition of his youth and inspired by the world of the nineteenth century as he knew it. Sometimes the themes and even the characters of the novels are brought into poems. The two genres run close together in subjects and attitudes, but the style of his poetry looks towards the more direct mediation of experience characteristic of this century, and away from the romantic recollection and refining of emotion more typical of most of his contemporaries. He came to know many of the younger poets and some of them acknowledged that they had learned from him.

Hardy also wrote a long epic drama, based on the Napoleonic Wars. Attempts have been made to stage *The Dynasts*, which came out between 1903 and 1908, but it is essentially a work for reading. Some of the scenes are almost naturalistic, though written in verse form. Others are allegorical, and introduce speakers like the Spirit of the Years and the Pities. The events of that period, which had always fascinated Hardy, serve as a broad commentary on human life. The force of destiny and the inevitable sweep of time, often presented in his novels, are now brought into more direct statements of philosophy. It is a work of bold conception. Its length and a certain portentousness in some of the choruses can make it tedious in long reading, but it contains much of the finest poetry that he wrote. It conveys a great vision, not always clearly verbalised, but with enough to show a powerful mind looking into the depths of human experience.

With the death of his mother at the age of ninety in 1904, the world of old Wessex must have seemed finally lost. Hardy was coming to be regarded as the Grand Old Man of English Letters rather than as the rebellious sceptic. He was awarded the Order of Merit in 1910 and seemed to be moving towards a quiet old age with little more to say. The death of his wife in 1912 was a trauma that reinvigorated his poetry. Sorrow and some remorse for the years of coldness between them moved him to revisit the places of their courtship and of Emma's early life. The result was a spate of poems, some telling directly of past years and some more obliquely recalling a lost love and a sterile marriage, which are among his finest pieces.

In 1914 he married Florence Emily Dugdale, thirty-eight years younger than himself, who had been helping with his work. His second marriage could never hope to recover the passion of youth, but it brought him domesticity and some happiness. Florence was inclined to depression and sometimes to jealousy, but Hardy in old age took these things more serenely. The outbreak of the Great War shook his belief, seen in *The Dynasts*, that humanity was slowly climbing towards a better future. He met with other eminent writers to consider how they could best help the national effort, but he also wrote poems on the futility of war. One, showing brotherhood with the German people through similarities between German and the Dorset dialect, caused offence to the intensely patriotic.

The final years were quiet. He continued to write poetry almost to the time of his death on 11 January 1928. A state funeral was granted, and leading writers of the day were among the pall-bearers when his ashes were buried in Westminster Abbey. But his last scene was linked to his first by an act which could well have appeared in one of his own novels or poems. His heart was removed from his body and buried in the grave of his first wife in Stinsford churchyard.

In the figurative sense, his heart had never really left the county which he had known in childhood and early youth. In creating 'Wessex' for his imaginative work, Hardy had created an enduring country of the mind. One of his great strengths is the feeling of reality in the places and experiences on which he drew and the characters he developed. We feel that we have known Hardy's people and that their lives are part of a true chronicle. Yet his work goes beyond the limits of time and place, to offer that deeper understanding of humanity, and so of ourselves, which only the greatest writers can give. No longer do critics label him simply as a pessimist or an atheist. His philosophy is not to be contained in any precise system. A few months before his death, preparing a new volume of poems for publication, he wrote, 'no harmonious philosophy is attempted in these pages – or in any bygone pages of mine, for that matter'. One thread which does seem to run through his work is that times of happiness are elusive and fleeting, and are therefore to be cherished; that love and friendship are fragile but among the most precious of human experiences.

There is much of the comedy of life as well as its tragedy, much of the quiet country life which was passing away even as he wrote of it. He was one of the greatest storytellers in our literature, bringing dignity to simple narratives without losing the sense of common reality. Above all, there is a deep compassion for those whom life has treated badly. His most memorable characters are sufferers, victims partly of their own weakness and partly of circumstances which we may choose to call Fate, or Chance, or leave unnamed. The world exacts its full penalty in the consequences of misfortunes and wrong choices; that is the essence of tragedy, and Hardy is a great tragic writer. As with all great tragedy, we read him and return to him not with depression of spirits, but with a renewed sense of the need to see life whole, and of the resources which enable us to meet it.

2 The Literary Background

Hardy's life was long, and he witnessed many changes in the world around him. His career as a novelist was comparatively short, covering the twenty-five years between 1871 and 1896. In 1918 he calculated that he had spent longer in writing poetry than in writing fiction. It was, however, as a novelist that he made his name, and the image of the great Victorian writer is essentially that of the novelist, just as it is of the poet in the Romantic period and of the dramatist in the Elizabethan. Yet to speak of 'the Victorian novel' is to suggest a singleness of purpose and execution which does not exist in reality. There are certain characteristics which recur frequently in fiction of the nineteenth century, but there is also great diversity and change.

It is in fact misleading to speak even of 'the Victorian age' without qualification. If we limit the period to the actual reign of Queen Victoria, we still have a stretch of sixty-four years – two clear generations. Britain in 1837 was in a different era from that of 1901. The details of changes fill volumes of history, but there are two broad areas which are important in their effect on the literature and thought of the time. One was the movement of the economy from being predominantly rural and based on the use of land to being industrial and manufacturing. The industrial revolution was well established at the beginning of the reign but the massive increase in production and transport came later. Secondly, it was a period of intellectual ferment, in which traditional beliefs were challenged and new theories offered in their place. Christianity was attacked from without and reconsidered from within; ideas of morality, the family and social class were also debated more widely than ever before. There was a third factor, which appears less overtly in literature but affected the whole nation: the power of central,

18

and later local, government over the individual increased year by year.

Most of those whom we regard as the great Victorian writers were adolescent or adult in 1837. The decade between 1810 and 1820 saw the birth of Dickens, Thackeray, Trollope, Kingsley, Eliot, the Brontës, Gaskell, Reade, Browning, Tennyson, Clough and Ruskin. Their formative years were those of George IV as Regent and then as King, and from those years they derived the presuppositions which they brought into the new reign. Hardy was of the next generation, yet born into a part of England which was then the least affected by change. Many of the seminal ideas and controversies developed when his mind was still open to novelty, but imbued with the simple faith of a peasant community. The paradoxes, and the consequent tension, make him unique among his contemporaries.

When Hardy published *Desperate Remedies* in 1871, the novel was a well-established and respected literary genre. Its status had not been easily achieved, and the objections which were made to some of Hardy's books showed that suspicion was not totally over-come. Dickens, who had died in the previous year, had done as much as any writer to make the novel both popular and esteemed. When he published his first novel in 1837, the situation had been different. The reading of fiction was opposed by Utilitarians who thought that it was a waste of time and a deviation from the serious learning of new knowledge and skills for the new age: the attitude of Mr Gradgrind which Dickens pilloried in *Hard Times*. It was opposed also by many moralists who believed that it put improper ideas into people's minds, gave them aspirations to rise above their station in life, and was objectionable because it depicted that which was untrue. Although Scott and a few others won grudging approval, fiction tended to be regarded as at best frivolous and at worst corrupting.

The struggle was largely won in the 1840s, while Hardy was growing up quietly at Higher Bockhampton. The unquestionable literary quality of Dickens, Thackeray and the Brontë sisters was supported by a steady increase in the desire to read, and the ability to do so. The appetite for books grew as educational opportunities expanded; the institutes set up to improve the literacy of working people ironically helped the novelists who were the objects of utili-tarian suspicion. In more privileged homes, the solidarity of the family circle and the absence of other amusements fostered both private reading and reading aloud in the evenings. The theatre was shunned by many of the respectable, and the current drama was not of a high standard. Circulating libraries, dominated by Mudie and Smith, made books more accessible in London, and by post to all parts of the country. Improved methods of production made books cheaper in relation to incomes, and many novels were presented in magazines or in separate monthly parts.

Hardy thus came to the art of fiction at a favourable time. Yet the very success of the novel brought its own difficulties. Too many people were trying their hand at the form and the market could not accommodate them all. Women, driven by boredom or financial need, could write novels without going out of their own homes. Anyone with a cause or theory at heart could use the novel to promulgate it; almost every movement for reform in the nineteenth century was accompanied by novels showing why it should be brought about, and others warning of the evil consequences if it were. Today we read and admire a few giants of the period, but a glance at old catalogues and publishers' lists reveals a multitude of forgotten names. These are only those who somehow got into print. In addition, the power of the circulating libraries was not entirely beneficent. They could, and did, impose their own censorship by refusing to stock novels which were considered to be immoral or in bad taste – and the level of tolerance was, by modern standards, very easily exceeded.

Neither popularity nor restraint prevented significant changes in the type of novel that was being written. Fiction had already shown itself able to accommodate social attitudes without loss of entertainment value. The novels of the 1850s and 60s were often earnest in respect of particular abuses and injustices. Increasingly, things were also being said about the deeper sickness in some aspects of the age, most notably in the later novels of Dickens. By the time Hardy started to write, the novel was considering also the new ideas and theories which that discontent had engendered. There was a new seriousness, a more intellectual approach, an ability to personify abstract thought within an imaginary structure. It was in 1859 that Darwin published *The Origin of Species* which generated shock or excitement in its first readers. In the same year George Meredith began his career as a serious novelist with *The Ordeal of Richard Feverel*, and George Eliot hers with *Adam Bede*. Not physical science alone was affecting people's minds; the social sciences were developing rapidly and could not be ignored. Sociology and psychology were beginning to use empirical methods and gaining credibility. Herbert Spencer, whose ideas Hardy admired, was writing before Darwin and continued to produce books until the last years of the century.

Earlier writers had understood intuitively the secrets of the human mind and had been able to put into words the way of life which they knew. Now the novelist felt it necessary to be acquainted with the new ideas and to draw them more specifically into fiction. The fashion of the novel was changing under the intellectual pressures, strengthened by the greater confidence of the new generation of novelists in their art. It was easier for them to make their own rules and to try to educate their readers without losing the quality of entertainment. From assurances that they did not corrupt innocence, they could now pass to a more positive assertion of their value to society.

After the middle of the century, the novel tended to portray life as it was being lived in the contemporary world. Just as the most popular painters were depicting domestic scenes suggesting a moment in a human story, the novelists held up a mirror to nature and helped people to an understanding of the real world and its problems. That, at least, was the theory behind realism; in practice it was not yet possible to look at the whole truth, and the controls exercised by the circulating libraries supported the inhibitions of the majority of readers. Nevertheless, the novel was being taken seriously by those who would once have dismissed it as trivial and untruthful. There was less fantasy, less poetry, less of the personal vision which had been exercised by Dickens.

The new fashion helped towards the success of Anthony Trollope and its later decline contributed to his posthumous loss of reputation. Trollope made the most of his talent by not attempting to go beyond what he could do well. Cautious and restrained in the dangerous areas of Victorian life, even he could be accused of too overt treatment of moral issues. He, more than any of his immediate contemporaries, gives a sense of the texture of life, set in an imaginative framework which makes it accessible and without losing the freedom of fiction. From the quiet Barchester novels to his later more serious explorations of political and financial circles, he managed to write over fifty novels in the course of a busy working life as a civil servant. He helped to destroy any lingering Romantic views of the writer as an artist waiting in for the moment of inspiration. He wrote for a set period every day, with a calculated number of words to be produced. He was the most successful example of the new image, the novelist as craftsman.

With domestic realism and didactic purpose, the novel might seem to have lost the capacity for sensation and excitement. In practice the appetite for these things was still fed by its practitioners. The old crude tradition of writing about crime and low life was given a new sense of respectability now that the novel had become a vehicle for social comment and reform. The novelist could get away with a great deal by honouring the ideal of the family and claiming to expose abuses. Sordid episodes were acceptable if the underlying principle was decent. Charles Reade gave his readers plenty of sensation by appealing to the social conscience. He could write highly charged and effective scenes, planned climaxes and emotional but telling dialogue, all stemming from his early experience as a dramatist and filling the place which the theatre had still left largely vacant. Wilkie Collins, a friend and collaborator of Dickens, treated the world of crime with a clever blend of the old melodrama and the new police organisation. Logical deduction and the patient following of clues were made to occupy the same plot.

Hardy was in this new fashion when he wrote *Desperate Remedies*. He never excluded the sensational even from his mature work and his novels contain many scenes which stand out pictorially and remain in the mind. Bathsheba looking at Fanny Robin and her baby in their coffin; Wildeve and Venn gambling by the light of glow-worms; Henchard looking on his own effigy in the water; Tess lying on the sacrificial stone at Stonehenge – these and many more are an aspect of his genius. He wrote of life as he knew it, but he also strove 'to reconcile the average with that uncommonness which alone makes it natural that a tale or experience would dwell in the memory and induce repetition'. He also knew that the writer must be a patient craftsman as well as an artist. 'It's important not to wait for the right mood', he wrote in his old age. 'If you do, it will come less and less'.

By the time that Hardy reached his success as a novelist, realism in fiction was moving towards naturalism. The name, and the idea, came from France, where Maupassant and Zola were trying to depict humanity objectively in fiction, as a phenomenon in the natural world. All events were seen as equally important for the record, and people were to be shown in the environment which determined what they were and how they acted. The basic evolutionary drives for survival and propagation were their motivation, and nothing in the realm of human experience should be deliberately omitted from the novel. Naturalism never became an integral part of the artistic climate of Britain to the extent that it did in France. Nor was it followed as a consistent theory even by those who claimed it. George Gissing tried honestly to depict what he saw as the basic sickness of his time and paid close attention to environmental influences. He wrote of those who had been given little previous attention in fiction, the lowest of the middle class, clinging to respectability but without security and always fearing the misfortune which would throw them into the abyss of total poverty. George Moore wrote of human degradation, of alcoholism and illegitimacy, with a precision of detail which had been denied to writers earlier in the century. Even in the 1880s it was too much for the circulating libraries and some of his books suffered their unofficial but effective suppression.

Hardy was never actually banned, but he sometimes had to make concessions to editors and publishers and he was required to change some of his wording. He resented the charge of obscenity and immorality which followed him throughout his career as a novelist. In 1890 he joined the current arguments about what was permissible with an essay 'Candour in English Fiction'. In the true vein of naturalism he wrote:

Life being a physiological fact, its honest portrayal must be largely concerned with, for one thing, the relations of the sexes, and the substitution for such catastrophes as favour the false colouring best expressed by the regulation finish that 'they married and were happy ever after', of catastrophes based upon sexual relations as it is.

Two years previously, he had complained of readers who 'so twist plain and obvious meanings as to see in an honest picture of human nature an attack on religion, morals, or institutions'. He knew and liked Gissing, inviting him to stay at Max Gate. His relationship with Moore was less amicable, and he was distressed by the attack on him which Moore made in *Conversations in Ebury Street*. Hardy himself wrote of poverty, sexual disasters, unhappy marriages, cruelty and violent death. He described in minute detail the working and domestic lives of country people, and he examined the effects on character of heredity, environment and circumstance.

Yet he is not to be labelled a realist or a naturalist without qualification. He was a poet, which Gissing was not at all, and Moore indifferently. His vision in the great novels is poetic and he makes universal significance from events which in the plain recital would seem limited and temporary. It is interesting that he quotes from very few contemporary novelists, but extensively from poets of all ages, including his own. He also had a profound sense of history, and the paradox of the individual's triviality and significance within it. His opinion of Zola, so admired by the British naturalists, was that he was an impressive social reformer, but 'no artist, and too material'.

Hardy was in fact overtly critical of the extremes to which realism in the novel might lead. In 1888 he wrote slightingly of writers whose characters use the current idiom and slang accurately, who 'lift their tea-cups or fan themselves to date' but who, in writing of what is ephemeral, 'have almost surely missed better things'. In another essay he said something which is undoubtedly true and is the answer to all claims to pure naturalism in literature:

> The most devoted apostle of realism, the sheerest naturalist, cannot escape, any more than the withered old gossip over her fire, the exercise of art in his labour or pleasure of telling a tale.

It was his ability to identify with the withered old gossip that gave Hardy much of his strength as a storyteller. Unlike the realists and naturalists, he offered few criticisms of specific abuses, and few appeals for specific reform. He saw much that was wrong, but his quarrel was with the human condition rather than with the details of contemporary society. His own experience made him a critic of the marriage laws and an advocate of divorce, and he was strong for the protection of animals from cruelty. But on the whole he was closer to the earlier Victorian novelists who sought remedies not in legislation but in the individual change of heart.

Hardy combined many of the characteristics of his contemporaries without conforming to a single pattern. He has the sensationalism and mystery of Reade and Collins, the sombre and even sordid treatment of Moore and Gissing, the moral earnestness and intellectual questioning of Eliot and Meredith. Earlier reviewers often compared him to George Eliot, but usually for their common treatment of peasant life and speech rather than for any shared mental attitudes. He brought to his novels his own deep sense of the past and the continuity of time, his memory of folk tales and ballads, and a real love for those who peopled his fiction.

His particular achievement was to raise the regional novel to a height not achieved before or since. The type was developing, partly influenced by the increased knowledge of hitherto remote parts of the country, brought about by the rapid development of public transport. The metropolitan dominance of London was still there, but it was less absolute. Novels were being written about particular and identifiable regions, in which the setting, characters, speech and general atmosphere were local. The regional novel is not written by simply stating that the story takes place in a certain area. Trollope created the delightful county of Barsetshire, but he wrote mostly of clerical and professional people who speak with standard accents and are at ease in London whenever the railway takes them there. The Brontës, especially Emily, had done something more distinctive with their native Yorkshire. Elizabeth Gaskell had written with careful attention to detail about industrial Lancashire and, in *Sylvia's Lovers*, about the north-east in an earlier period. Their work was quite different in effect from the rural excursions of Smollett, Fielding and Austen, or the brief and uncertain forays outside London made by Dickens. Walter Scott alone had consistently though not invariably, written about a particular part of Britain. Whether Scotland can properly be called a 'region' is a doubtful and perhaps tendentious question, and it might be more accurate to regard him as a national novelist.

Hardy wrote about a region that was unquestionably part of England and which, although in many ways pursuing its own way of life, was inextricably caught up in the affairs of the whole. Unlike Scott, he wrote almost always about contemporary or recent history and depicted a way of life which he had directly experienced. The counties which make up his Wessex are real and identifiable. The centre of most of his action is in Dorset, and he never moves further north than Oxford, further west than eastern Cornwall or further east than Wiltshire. He sometimes uses real place-names, but more often disguises actual places under invented names. Although he discouraged attempts to make detailed identification, most of his descriptions are accurate and easily related to actual places. He drew a map of the area covered in the novels but 'rather unwillingly . . . owing to the constant inquiries of readers for the actual places'.

He took the setting of his fiction seriously and wished the title 'Wessex Novels' to be used in advertising. In the preface to a later edition of *Far from the Madding Crowd* he wrote:

> I ventured to adopt the word 'Wessex' from the pages of early English history, and give it a fictitious significance as the existing name of the district once included in that extinct kingdom. The series of novels I projected being mainly of the kind called local, they seemed to require a territorial definition of some sort to lend unity to their scene.

He told a correspondent that Wessex was not simply Dorset but was 'coterminous with the Wessex of History' though he admitted that 'by far the most numerous scenes lie in the portion called "South Wessex" i.e. Dorset'. His great achievement was to create a world which, while rooted in reality, allowed the full development of imagination. Today one can trace the events of the novels and stories through towns and villages. 'Wessex' is also a country of the mind, as James Joyce created infinite variety in a Dublin which is yet marked with precision. Hardy was concerned that his work should not be read as only the quaint record of a distinct way of life which was vanishing. In the general preface to the Wessex Edition of 1912 he wrote that his characters were intended as 'beings in whose hearts and minds that which is apparently local should be universal'.

One of the distinctive features of the region was its dialect, already threatened by change and conformity together with other aspects of rural life. Hardy's use of dialect is an important part of his contribution to literary language and will be considered in detail later. He was by no means the first to attempt the representation of local or non-standard speech in writing. Chaucer and Shakespeare give special forms to characters whose speech has regional features, and the early novelists of the eighteenth century use deviant spelling for rustic characters like Fielding's Squire Western. It was Scott above all who first tackled the problem seriously and tried to differentiate between different levels and intensities of Scots. As the regional novel gained popularity, writers had the problem of using the regular alphabet and devices of punctuation to accommodate sounds of particular dialects. The balance between showing difference and keeping intelligibility was delicate, and not always maintained. Emily Brontë frequently tips it against the reader in *Wuthering Heights*, particularly in the speech of Joseph. Even her sister Charlotte's revisions for the second edition did not always restore clarity. Elizabeth Gaskell used Lancashire dialect in *Mary Barton* and *North and South*, with careful attention to detail and even footnotes to explain the provenance of certain words. In *Sylvia's Lovers* nearly all the dialogue is cast in the form of the north Yorkshire dialect. Dickens excelled in the use of rich, if idiosyncratic, cockney; it is impossible to think of Sam Weller or Mrs Gamp without their phonic deviations as well as their private turns of phrase. He was not so fully successful with other regional accents.

Hardy came into a literary inheritance which granted dialect a place in fiction. The novelists who immediately preceded him had extended sub-standard speech from comic or melodramatic characters and given it the status of serious events. Mrs Gaskell's John Barton and Dickens's Stephen Blackpool can rise to dignity and arouse our compassion in speeches that are set down with deviant spelling. There was also a considerable amount of work by writers who used their own natural dialect to relate local happenings or as a vehicle for social protest. The ballad tradition survived into the age of literacy, seldom of great artistic merit, but often moving and compelling. Dialect was to be found also in the work of some contemporary poets. Tennyson wrote pieces in the Lincolnshire dialect of his childhood; Outram used the dialect of Glasgow, and T. E. Brown that of the Isle of Man.

In the matter of written dialect, the most important example for Hardy was William Barnes. Born in Dorset in 1801 and educated at Cambridge, Barnes was for many years headmaster of a school in Dorchester. Hardy might well have studied under him if his parents had not preferred to keep him with Isaac Last. Later, Barnes became rector of a Dorset parish. He had early aspirations to become a dramatist but failure to get a start in the theatre turned him to poetry. He wrote mainly in the Dorset dialect, using elaborate forms of spelling and resources of punctuation, including the diaresis, for local vowel sounds. Hardy came to know him, and had a high regard for his poetry. He reviewed a volume by Barnes in 1879, wrote his obituary for the *Athenaeum* in 1886 and introduced a posthumous collection of poems in 1909.

This long attachment to the work of Barnes was more than objective admiration. Hardy's poetry owes a great deal to Barnes, and so indeed does the dialect element in the novels. As will be seen later, Hardy's method of representation was deliberately less elaborate and more accessible. He did not attempt to secure an accurate and consistent realisation of Dorset speech, and one of his few criticisms of Barnes was the occasionally opaque quality of the poems – as difficult to penetrate as Emily Brontë's showing of Yorkshire speech. From Barnes Hardy derived the belief that Dorset dialect had the status of an old system of language in its own right and should not be considered merely a deviation from a new national standard. It was with this conviction that he brought rustic conversation into his poems and novels, and invested it with the dignity of his total vision. Barnes also strengthened his wider interest in the life and folklore of Dorset, and showed how simple subject-matter was not incompatible with experiments in metres and stanza forms. In other ways, however, the two men were different. Barnes retained the faith of his youth, and a certain optimism despite his ability to record sadness. Barnes was essentially a man of the early century, untouched by the controversies of the Victorian age.

Barnes was an influence on Hardy, even though the latter's poetry developed along a very different course. He was perhaps the only poet of whom the word 'influence' can be used with any confidence. All poets owe something to predecessors and contemporaries, but the degree of direct influence varies greatly and it is too easy to find influence in likeness derived from a common non-literary source. The Victorian period produced a great deal of poetry, and a few really great poets, but it was not a predominantly poetic age. There was no sustained thrust of poetic enthusiasm, and no major school of shared ideals and principles comparable to that of the period which was ending when Victoria came to the throne. Hardy did not espouse any of the lesser movements which created fashions in poetry during his lifetime. He was untouched by the Spasmodics, the Pre-Raphaelites and the Aesthetes. He did, however, regard poetry as a higher form of literature than the novel, even though his fame during the nineteenth century was almost entirely won through fiction. In his preface to the 1912 edition of his novels, he remarked 'how much more concise and quintessential expression becomes when given in rhythmic form than when shaped in the language of prose'. As early as 1888, after the great achievement of *The Mayor of Casterbridge*, he wrote to a correspondent, 'It sometimes occurs to me that it is better to fail in poetry than to succeed in prose'.

He certainly had a wide familiarity with the poets, both of the past and of his own time. He quotes a great deal of poetry in his novels and stories, usually to emphasise a situation or a comment. He thought very highly of Browning and shows signs of his admiration in his development of the dramatic monologue as a poetic form, and perhaps in his prosodic experiments. He was very far from sharing Browning's famous 'optimism' about life, though it should never be forgotten that Browning was full of the questionings of his time and was capable of being savage and even gloomy in his poetry. On the whole, the two men thought very differently about things in general. Hardy quoted Tennyson frequently, but did not come under his poetic spell. His use of the stanza form of *In Memoriam* for the totally different response of 'A Sign Seeker' is perhaps indicative of how he regarded Tennyson as a thinker, even though he enjoyed the poetry itself.

He used a number of lines by Swinburne, especially in his later books, praised Swinburne's poetry, and wrote a moving elegy for him in 'A Singer Asleep'. The admiration was perhaps more for Swinburne's generally rebellious attitude, and his liberating effect on some of the younger generation of the time, than for his actual execution. Hardy's feeling that both of them had suffered from hostile criticism, based on content rather than quality, also helped the fellow-feeling. He met Matthew Arnold and shared with him moods of reflection and anxiety about the tensions of the new emerging world. There is little sign of poetic influence, although 'Dover Beach' is perhaps of all Victorian poems closest to Hardy's thinking.

Of earlier poets, Wordsworth had his effect, as he had upon so many poets of the Victorian age. Hardy, like Wordsworth, could use absolute simplicity to great effect; he could also allow it to entrap him into bathos. 'The Self-Unseeing' is an example of the former, 'The Slow Nature' of the latter. Behind Wordsworth, as behind many English poets, stands an older tradition, the popular ballad. Hardy in his childhood knew it still in its oral form, and it was this rather than any of its literary revivals that he brought to his poetry. He comes closer to the folk simplicity of theme and treatment than the deliberate mediaevalists like William Morris; only A. E. Housman at his best equals him in this. The ballad quality of human values in basic living, of timeless experience and of supernatural presence, can be found in many of his poems. Examples are: 'During Wind and Rain', 'A Sunday Morning Tragedy' and 'Who is in the next room?' There are many echoes of other voices in Hardy's poetry, but as he moves into the twentieth century his voice becomes distinctively his own.

All writers, whatever their individual genius or their literary influences, must draw upon the common usage of their time. There is no way of gaining a hearing if originality is stretched beyond the limits of shared communication. A writer may indeed add to the language and, in times of rapid change, even help to influence its course. At the same time he will be constrained by what is possible in the speech of his contemporaries, a complex system to which even the greatest writers can contribute only a little.

By the middle of the nineteenth century English had long been fixed in grammatical structure and in the conventions of an agreed spelling. The interest of the regional novel depended partly on the national acceptance of a standard form for writing and the belief that a certain mode of speech, albeit a minority one, represented an educated standard. The same assumptions apply today, although they are often challenged; they did not apply through centuries of earlier development. The modern reader meets few difficulties in Hardy with regard to normal grammar and vocabulary. The stylistic habits and inventions which made his language distinctive were mostly as notable in his own time as they are now.

A few features which were normal a hundred years ago have disappeared or become rare. The use of the subjunctive for doubt and hypothesis is now uncommon in writing, almost extinct in speech except for a few stock phrases like 'as it were'. The proper use of *whom* is moribund and the preservation of the nominative in statements like 'it is I' is virtually extinct. Things which now seem pedantic would not very long ago have been neglected at the peril of the user's being considered incorrect. Occasionally the reader may be surprised by a difference in auxiliary verbs; the verb *to be* could be used with certain verbs, as when Hardy writes in *Jude the Obscure*, 'the idlers . . . were all gone now'.

Vocabulary tends to change more rapidly than grammar. The main feature of the nineteenth century in word usage is the great influx of new words to express new inventions, discoveries and ideas. This process has continued in the twentieth century and is unlikely to decrease. Few words have become completely obsolete over the last hundred years, and it is safe to say that the average native speaker of English has a larger vocabulary – perhaps much of it passive rather than active – than his or her counterpart among Hardy's contemporaries. When Hardy uses a rare, recondite or old-fashioned word, the problem for the modern reader generally existed in his own time. Occasional difficulties can usually be resolved through one of the older dictionaries. Even in *Jude the Obscure*, the last of the novels, we may be halted for a moment by a comparison of two intellects 'as a star to a benzoline lamp' or by a reference to a 'mechanical tell-tale of monies received' in a public house. The understanding that *benzoline* was a liquid fuel and a *tell-tale* an early type of cash register should not be long in coming.

A word still in common use may have changed, extended or restricted its meaning. When the elderly Geoffrey Day speaks of his wife as 'mother-in-law' we may be puzzled until we learn that the phrase could then mean 'stepmother' and that he refers to his second wife's relationship to his daughter. There is a more serious problem in the changing associations of words and phrases as used in conversation. Titles, names and the choice of vocabulary could show social attitudes and personal feelings with a subtlety which has largely been lost in modern usage. The whole question of what is known as *register* is something that needs more detailed treatment in a later chapter. When Hardy's dialogue seems to be stilted, the fault may lie with the difference between polite usage then and now. He was extremely sensitive to speech, both formal and colloquial. However, his judgement does sometimes fail and the artificiality of some passages derives partly from a personal lapse and partly from the conventions of contemporary fiction. It was understood that virtuous or centrally interesting characters should speak 'good' English, even if their environment did not provide it. Dialect was becoming acceptable for serious characters, but the place of Tess and Jude in their stories does not allow for the type of speech which would be more realistic. Dickens had dealt in the same way with characters like Oliver Twist and Lizzie Hexam.

In general, the attitude of writers and educators towards the language was still prescriptive. Generations of grammarians and lexicographers had established 'rules' for English, based on Latin categories and regarded as essential for the educated writer and speaker. The arrival of sub-standard speech in fiction and a more colloquial tone in poetry did not mean any relaxation of criteria for careful usage. Hardy and his contemporaries respected the grammar book and the dictionary when they were writing narrative or description. Standards of English were still almost entirely text centred, with the great writers of the past as 'authorities'.

There were a few whose concern for the primitive purity of English made them desire to rid the language of its Romance element and develop a Saxon-derived vocabulary. William Barnes was the most fervent of the Saxonists, and was prepared to take the matter further than the occasional revivals and coinages of William Morris, and the limited enthusiasm of Dickens, who wrote an article claiming that 'our best authors, except Milton, have all been maintainers of Saxon'.[1] Barnes wrote several books on the subject, the last with the title *An Outline of Rede-Craft*. He wanted to replace 'conscience' by *inwit*, 'aqueduct' by *water-lode*, 'quadrangular' by *fourwinkled*, 'genealogy' by *kinlore*, and a great many others. He found some support but more opposition; Hardy coined a number of Saxonisms, but even more Latinisms, and searched the extremes of the English vocabulary for his purpose. In his obituary of Barnes, he recalled the old man objecting to 'bicycle' and wanting to say *wheel-saddle*.

The idiosyncrasy of Barnes was just an extreme form of

a growing interest in English, and in the study of language in general. Earlier work on Sanskrit and primitive Germanic forms had made the comparative study of languages possible. The Philological Society was founded in 1841. Work began on the *New English Dictionary*, with its concern for changing usage and definitions based on specific examples – Samuel Johnson had pointed the way, but without the resource of nation-wide contributors. Henry Sweet struck the first decisive blow against the dominance of Latin categories with his *New English Grammar* in 1892. Serious work on English dialects was led by Joseph Wright, with whom Hardy corresponded about Dorset speech, and Alexander John Ellis. The pioneers of modern phonological and linguistic study were Hardy's contemporaries. He created his novels and poems from his own ear, memory and reading; but he lived through the years when the skills necessary to record and describe living English were being developed.

3 Hardy and the English Language

The most important evidence for the use of language by Hardy, or by any other writer, is the whole body of his work. His own ideas about style, and his replies to critics, are also of interest in preparing an approach to his fiction and poetry; the judgement of others upon his work can suggest further lines of investigation but should not be used as a ready-made structure for evaluation. In order that we may begin with an open mind, consider these statements:

Mr. Hardy disfigures his pages by bad writing, by clumsy and inelegant metaphors, and by mannerism and affectation.

Mr. Hardy's style can now be recognized as his own, and as one of the best in English fiction.

As we read this curious and wearisome volume, these many slovenly, slipshod, uncouth verses, stilted in sentiment, poorly conceived and wrought, our respect lessens to vanishing-point.

Neither in verse nor in prose is Mr. Hardy a master of style.

A style which is at once recognized as individual in its simplicity, its strength, its grace.

Poor stuff, poetically – Johnsonian in heaviness of thought, and sesquipedalian in verbal expression.

Mr. Hardy's volume . . . is full of poetry; and yet it is also full of ugly and cumbrous expressions, clumsy metres, and flat, prosaic turns of speech.

No style in literature, save Scott's, is so difficult to analyse; it is on the face of it so bad, yet it achieves its aim so unmistakably.

The problem of Hardy's style is its inconsistency.[1]

These brief extracts from many criticisms in Hardy's own lifetime and later, reveal a degree of contradiction and uncertainty which is rare in dealing with an undoubtedly great writer. They reveal also the fact that Hardy's use of language is not to be summed up in a few succinct sentences. He did not write in the plain tradition of English prose mastered by Swift and Hazlitt among others, which is so easy to read and so hard to emulate. Nor is his style marked by idiosyncrasies which are frequent and predictable enough to make it instantly recognisable and open to parody, like that of Carlyle or Morris or much of Dickens. Yet, like all writers, he has distinguishing features and tricks which are particularly his own. They have to be discovered, and their effect assessed, as they occur in verse and prose. There is little in Hardy which can be found constantly and with even distribution, either by periods of his life or the genre in which he was writing a given text. The puzzlement of the critics is summed up in the last quotation given: but is it 'inconsistency' in a negative sense, or is it a richness which draws without inhibition on every resource of English?

Both factors are present in the complex totality of Hardy's style. The word 'style' itself is debatable and may be used in different ways. The judgements of critics show that it can be approached evaluatively, with opinions based on individual views of what constitutes 'good writing'. It is in this sense that we often speak loosely of an author's style, using criteria based on the work of others as well as on a prescriptive notion of the 'rules' of English. This is by no means a worthless exercise; but it is important to think of style also as something which is open to more objective analysis and description of how the writer uses the language available. Choice of words from the contemporary lexis of the language, arrangement of clauses, unusual word order to 'foreground' a phrase by bringing it into prominence – these are only a few of the features which need to be examined in a survey of style. The evaluation of quality, with increased understanding and appreciation, should rest on technical assessment rather than on the reaction of pleasure or distaste to a single work or to isolated passages.

Hardy has generally been considered a careless writer, whose use of language falls short of his genius as a tragic novelist. He has been accused of the unnecessary use of rare and recondite words, of involved and untidy sentence construction, and of a general lack of decorum in haphazardly mixing the learned and the colloquial, the simple and the complex. A study of his work shows that he is not free from these and other faults, but it also reveals stylistic qualities which match his total achievement in literature. Language is the writer's raw material, and greatness cannot be found where there is incompetence in its use. Not all our leading writers were great stylists, but to create something unique and memorable out of the linguistic resources available is the qualification for literary status. Hardy may not always have used English with full discrimination, but his acknowledged power of creating character, writing scenes of natural description, and touching some of the deepest points of human experience, did not come with disregard for language.

It is, however, true that he was more concerned with theme and approach in literature than with the minutiae of style. He tended to believe that the right intention would produce the right effect. It was part of the Romantic legacy to emphasise the substance rather than the form; in 1881 Hardy observed:

Style – consider the Wordsworthian dictum (the more perfectly the natural object is reproduced, the more truly poetic the picture). This reproduction is achieved by seeing into the *heart of a thing* (as rain, wind, for instance), and is realism, in fact, though through being pursued by means of the imagination it is confounded with invention, which is pursued by the same means.   (*EL* 189)

His involvement in his stories and his sympathy with his characters sometimes caused him to overlook faults of expression. It is, however, certain that he was neither insensitive nor indifferent to the language in which his life's work was written.

His extensive use of dialect is one proof of his linguistic skill, and requires detailed treatment later. He valued Dorset speech as an ancient and noble form of English and he was always ready to defend it against dismissal or misunderstanding. In later life he corresponded with dialectologists, was careful to explain the nuances of local speech to translators of his work, and regretted the gradual decline of the old forms. He was not, however, a narrow antiquarian and he did not follow the extreme form of linguistic nationalism advocated by Barnes, from whom he learned so much in other ways. He cared for the concept of good English as a whole and wanted to guard the language against error and contamination.

He supported the Society for Pure English, and became a vice-president of the English Association when it was formed in 1906. As late as 1922 he was writing to Robert Bridges, the then Poet Laureate, about the deficiencies of the old grammar books and wondering where a student could find clear guidance about such problems as the split infinitive and whether the relative pronoun 'should be in the same case as the antecedent, or only in the same gender and number' (*CL* VI 125). This is not the mark of a man ignorant or careless about English; the less prescriptive mood of the present age may even consider it too fussy. He was interested in spelling reform and approved the system of transcription used in the *Oxford English Dictionary*, 'though it might be improved in some respects' (*CL* V 97). As he grew older he was inclined, like many others, to believe that the standard of English was deteriorating. He disliked neologisms like *cablegram* ('illegitimate word!') and found that 'the increasing influx of American journals, fearfully and wonderfully worded, helps on the indifference to literary form' (*PW* 147). Literature in the early twentieth century seemed 'to be losing its qualities as an art, and to be assuming a structureless and conglomerate character'.

His views on style were not merely negative. He believed that it was a quality which each individual writer must develop through 'his personal eyes, and in his peculiar moods', and that deep feeling and sincerity should be 'unhampered by considerations of nice collocation and balance of sentences, still less by conventionally accepted examples' (*PW* 122). About 1875, early in his career as a novelist, he was reading extensively 'in a study of style' and decided that he was:

More and more confirmed in an idea which I have long
held as a matter of common sense, long before I thought
of any old aphorism bearing on the subject; 'Ars est celare
artem'. The whole secret of a living style and the difference
between it and a dead style, lies in not having too much style
– being, in fact, a little careless, or rather seeming to be, here
and there . . . Otherwise your style is like worn half-pence –
all the fresh image rounded off by rubbish, and no crispness
at all. (*EL* 138).

The carelessness for which Hardy has been censured by
so many critics may be seen as a conscious avoidance of the
artificial and too 'literary' precision of some writers. He certainly
owed a lot to his own fine ear for speech and other sounds, even
though that ear could occasionally fail him. Yet he read much,
over a wide range of literary and non-literary works. A writer
is inevitably influenced by what he reads, though the amount of
conscious imitation varies among individuals. We know a lot about
Hardy's reading, from his notebooks and letters as well as from
the many allusions in his work. He read Bunyan and Lytton as
a boy, Spenser, Shakespeare, Burns, Byron, Wordsworth, Scott,
Shelley and Tennyson during his first years in London. A little
later he was reading Thackeray and Macaulay, Milton, Darwin
and Huxley. The list could be extended; it is enough to reveal
a mind omnivorous for literature and thought, wide in sympathy
and not limited by prejudice for or against any period of history.
He came to regard Gibbon as a writer whose style had always
delighted him, but he could also admire Newman, who is one of
the writers listed as read for the 'study of style' quoted above.
The Authorised Version of the Bible seemed to him a model of
good simplicity.

Of his contemporaries, Matthew Arnold was an influence on his
thought but less so on his writing. He entered into a discussion of
style with Arnold but was not pleased with the latter's opinion that
Swift was 'the best man to read for style' (*EL* 175). Reading Henry
James confirmed his own inclination towards studied carelessness:
'after this kind of work, one feels inclined to be purposely careless
in detail' (*EL* 277). He had a great regard for French writers, who
seemed to him both to write well and to be free from many of the
encumbrances and inhibitions prevailing in England, and he knew

something of French literature from Rabelais to Anatole France. He was not so impressed by Zola, to whom he was sometimes compared, and once said that Crabbe brought realism into English literature half a century before Zola. Recalling this remark years later, he was careful to add that his own 'art of writing . . . was influenced far more by Shakespeare, Shelley, Browning, etc. than by Crabbe' (*CL* V 294).

The impression is of a writer who, despite his later assertion and practice of independence, was subject at first to divers literary influences. He was perhaps liable to direct imitation, though never deliberately playing the 'sedulous ape' in the careful cultivation of style as Stevenson and others have done. His early mentor, Horace Moule, gave him much advice on reading but warned him, 'you must in the end write *your own* style, unless you would be a mere imitator'. Leslie Stephen, who took over some of Moule's function towards Hardy, gave him advice which fitted his own inclination:

> I should think the less you bother yourself about critical canons the less chance there is of your becoming self-conscious and cramped. I should, therefore, advise the great writers – Shakespeare, Goethe, Scott, etc. etc., who give ideas and don't prescribe rules.[2]

It was advice which Hardy was later prepared to give to others; asked for a contribution to a volume about writing he replied:

> Any detailed rules as to the formation of style I could not possibly give, for I know of none that are of practical utility. A writer's style is according to his temperament, and my impression is that if he has anything to say which is of value, and words to say it with, the style will come of itself. (*CL* I 168)

Perhaps that last assertion throws some light on both the strengths and the weaknesses of Hardy's own writing.

Although he proclaimed and took an independent line in writing, Hardy was extremely sensitive to criticisms of his work. He felt that he was unjustly accused of being coarse, obscene and irreligious, and this troubled him even more than comments on the quality of his language. He found that his opinions could be expressed more freely in poetry than in fiction; the discovery confirmed his preference for verse, which seemed to him a more satisfying form, and one capable of greater precision in the record of emotion. In the preface to the 1912 revised edition of his novels he observed 'how much more precise and quintessential expression becomes when given in rhythmic form than when shaped in the language of prose'. In the same year he declared that 'the shortest way to good prose is by the route of good verse':

> Anybody may test it for himself by taking any fine lines in verse and, casting off the forms of metre and rhyme that seems to bind the poet, trying to express the same ideas more freely and accurately in prose. He will find that it cannot be done: the words of the verse – fettered as he thought them – are the only words that will convey the ideas that were intended to be conveyed. (*PW* 147)

His movement from prose fiction to poetry did not put an end to adverse criticism of his language. His diction was regarded as rough and even barbarous, a charge which became less frequent as Victorian expectations shaded into the modern style. He had no doubt of the rightness of his approach. He desired from his first attempts at verse to avoid the 'jewelled line', which he regarded as 'effeminate'. He thought of his writing as a style in which 'the nature of the finish may be bold rather than minute – like a drawing on a paper with a rough surface' (*CL* V 249). That is a good image, as later discussion of his style will show; poems which at first appear almost uncouth prove on close reading to be the work of a man who had a fine ear for sound and a sense of the vital structure of English. The modern departure from traditional prosody did not generally please him. In much free verse:

> There is no expectation raised of a response in sound or beat, and the pleasures of its gratification, as in regular poetry: which only ancient poetry, like the English Bible, is able to dispense with, because of its other character of antiquity. (*CL* V1 186)

There have been few writers so innovative as Hardy who have also been so deeply rooted in regard for tradition.

His sensitivity to criticism was expressed both in public

utterances and in private. He accused reviewers of 'the old game of sampling the poem or drama by quoting the worst line or passage only' (*PW* 56). What he had written in his early years about the virtues of deliberate apparent carelessness, and the art which conceals art remained part of his creed as a writer. In 1919, when the greater part of his work had been done, he claimed that reviewers:

> Do not know that dissonances, and other irregularities can be produced advisedly as art, and worked as to give more charm than strict conformities, to the mind and ear of those trained and steeped in poetry; but they assume that a poet who commits one of these irregularities does so because of his ignorance, and the inferiority of his ear to that of the critic himself. *Ars est celare artem* they have never heard of or forget it. (*CL* V 345)

He had been faithful to his opinion for nearly forty-five years; the judgement upon it lies in what he wrote and the response of each new reader. Enough has been said to show that his style, whether good or bad, was not the result of indifference. Apart from his overt statements about language and style, his deep knowledge of English literature ensured that his innovations were built upon a sense of continuity; the instrument which lay to his hand in the second half of the nineteenth century was one which generations of writers had used and helped to create.

He constantly drew upon that great tradition, by direct allusion and by more subtle influences which appear in both verse and prose. Perhaps he valued above all the basic simplicity of English literary language, the homeliness and the lyricism which has almost entirely excluded the sense of a 'high style' well removed from everyday discourse. We do not associate Hardy particularly with the Elizabethan age; but his response to the lyrical poetry of that period was deep and lasting. Recalling his early reading he wrote, 'Lodge's poem to Rosaline was one of the few which awakened me to a true, or mature, consciousness of what poetry consists in' (*CL* I 122). At the end of his life, his memory went back to the same era and the same style. His second wife wrote:

> His only ambition, so far as he could remember, was to have some poem or poems in a good anthology like the

Golden Treasury. The model he had set before him was 'Drink to me only', by Ben Jonson.   (*LY* 263)

In his end was his beginning: simplicity was the keynote, in style as in a vanished way of life, but it was the simplicity of the profound, not of the ingenuous mind. That assertion must be tested by examining the many ways in which he drew on the resources of the English language. To learn what is characteristic of his style is a means towards fuller appreciation of his other qualities as a writer.

4   Language of Reading

The native speaker of any language communicates by selecting
and arranging items from the *lexis* or vocabulary of that language.
These items are traditionally called 'words'. Modern linguistic
theory has raised questions about the status and definition of a
'word' in a connected utterance: such questions can be important
and interesting, but they need not inhibit a discussion of Hardy's
language as a literary medium. Our normal perception of a word
tells us that we all continually perform these acts of selection and
arrangement, and that the creative writer performs them with
unusual care and skill. Most writers have a vocabulary that is
larger than the average, and draw on its resources in imaginative
and unexpected ways. There is in fact no 'average' vocabulary,
for the range varies with age, education and linguistic sensitivity.
However, most people can produce enough words to meet the
regular needs of their lives and can understand a larger number
than they actually use.[1]

If we think of a basic working vocabulary as a circle enclosing
a large number of words, we can also be aware of many other
circles within the total lexis of the language, each containing a
smaller number of words in more limited use, and we can label
these circles with titles; names like 'archaism', 'slang', 'jargon',
'dialect' and so on. The vocabulary of each individual will show
one or more of these circles cutting into it to some extent. A
young person will probably have a large section of the 'slang'
circle and little of the 'archaism'. Some speakers will have a
considerable area of 'dialect', others little or none (though we
should remember that what we consider the 'standard' form
of English is historically developed from a dialect). Writers of
literature are likely to know their way around many of these
smaller circles and to draw from them words which they might

not use as private individuals. Although a writer can take great liberties with vocabulary, and even invent new words or produce existing words in unusual combinations, the need to communicate to readers keeps most literary language within the area of shared agreement about words and their meanings.

A speech community usually develops different 'styles', used by groups sharing a common understanding or interest and marked by words and phrases which are not in general currency. The outsider learns to recognise these styles without using them. We know that Parliamentary style includes reference to 'honourable members on this side of the House'; legal to 'my learned friend'. There is no 'style' in this sense for the language of literature; we may have an idea that literature should be more 'correct' or 'careful' than everyday speech, but we do not on the whole react to particular usages as being literary in an exclusive sense. Some national cultures have developed a 'high style' for literature, but English literature has always been close to common usage, prepared for colloquial expressions and homely allusions when they are appropriate. The writer is free to draw on all styles, as on all personal modes of expression. The only criterion is the effectiveness of choice within the whole imaginative structure which creates a novel or play or poem.

The credibility of a character in a novel is much greater if dialogue contains words which seem appropriate to that character's supposed background and way of life. Hardy makes good use of this device, especially for characters who share some of his own knowledge or interests. Thus in the minor novel *A Laodicean*, George Somerset is an architect explaining features of an old castle to the woman who has bought it and with whom he is secretly in love:

> 'It is in this little arcade that the example occurs,' said Somerset.
> 'O yes,' she answered, turning to look at it.
> 'Early piers, capitals, and mouldings, generally alternated with deep hollows, so as to form strong shadows. Now look under the abacus of this capital; you will find the stone hollowed out wonderfully; and also in this arch-mould.'   (*AL* 116)

The reader who would not be sure of using these words correctly is given a sense that Somerset knows what he is talking about and his character grows stronger. Or the character may become real not through specialised knowledge, but through a response which the reader can fully share. Tess wants to express her happiness in song:

> She tried several ballads, but found them inadequate; till, recollecting the psalter that her eyes had so often wandered over of a Sunday morning before she had eaten of the tree of knowledge, she chanted: 'O ye Sun and Moon . . . O ye Stars . . . ye Green Things upon the Earth . . . ye Fowls of the Air . . . Beasts and Cattle . . . Children of Men . . . bless ye the Lord, praise Him and magnify Him for ever!' (*TD* 118)

Hardy's readers would have recognised the phrases of the *Benedicite*, often sung at Mattins. They would also of course have picked up the Biblical reference to 'the tree of knowledge'.

The lexis of English is unusually rich and extensive because of the mixing of words derived from Old English, the early Saxon form of the language, with words of Romance origin coming from Latin either directly or through French. In ordinary colloquial speech the proportion of Saxon words is higher than in more learned writing, but Old English provides the basis of vocabulary for all kinds of usage. Hardy was not a devoted Saxonist like William Barnes, and he drew on every type of word as he needed it. He does, however, sometimes use Saxon words which readers would recognise but not actively use. Thus dust can be called not white but *hoar*; a man's head is his *poll*; lack of understanding is not *trowing*; a densely wooded area is *bosky*. The incidence of such words is greatest in the poetry, with words such as *wot, ruth, wonning, yestreen* instead of the more familiar 'knows', 'pity', 'dwelling', 'yesterday evening'. The various Spirits in *The Dynasts* have a rather surprising partiality for such expressions as *what ye list, wots not of, they trow not, more boots it*.

Whether Hardy liked these words for their archaic flavour and sense of continuity from the past, or whether he used them to make a more surprising effect, cannot easily be determined. Sometimes the former is suggested, as in the phrase 'three hundred years hied'. The old word can seem totally right as in the lines:

The troubled skulls that heave
And fust in the flats of France   (*P* 727)

where the alliterating monosyllable *fust* is more striking than
the regular equivalents 'moulder' or 'decay' and gives an echo
of Hamlet's 'That capability and godlike reason/ To fust in us
unused'. It may be less satisfactory when the Saxon word
remains in use but the meaning has changed. It is easy to
misunderstand when Pierston's ideal woman is described as 'a
subjective phenomenon vivified by the weird influences of his
descent and birthplace' (*WB* 8), if we do not take *weird* in its
old sense of 'fateful' like Macbeth's 'weird sisters'. Saxon words
survive, often close to their original meanings, in the Dorset dialect. When Hardy depicts dialect speakers the incidence of such
words is naturally high and is decided by truth to life rather than
the deliberate archaism chosen in narrative passages.

Critics in his own time and later have been more severe
on Hardy for using rare words of Latin derivation. He does
sometimes seem to take pleasure in recondite words for their
own sakes, and to use them in passages where they conflict with
more natural and familiar expressions. It has been suggested that
his lack of formal education made him self-conscious about his
knowledge and that he wished to show himself as the equal of
writers with university backgrounds. This is not a convincing
explanation; Hardy received a better and longer education than
the majority of his contemporaries, and one which gave him a
good grounding in Latin on which he built by his own reading
with the guidance of Horace Moule. He had as much schooling
as Shakespeare, Dickens and Bernard Shaw. He lived in an
age when self-help and private learning were considered highly
commendable and there is no evidence of his feeling any sense
of inferiority.

The fact remains that his vocabulary is at times strongly
Latinate. He can use a Romance word where a Saxon one
would be more natural, as when he describes the moving shadows
thrown by the Sun on its 'diurnal roll' (*TD* 156) where 'daily'
would do very well, or when the end of a spoken utterance is
marked by the phrase, 'he said terminatively' (*TD* 121). There
is no need to call a fork in the road *bifurcation* (*JO* 244) or a
change of mind *tergiversation* (*PBE* 218). A sleepwalker is more

than once called a *noctambulist*, a newly-born creature *nascent*, a housebound life is *intramural existence*, underlying brightness a *substratum of radiance*. The reader does not need to be a Saxonist like Barnes to find these needlessly mannered in passages of simple and moving narrative.

Some of Hardy's Latinate words are rare enough to need a footnote in a modern edition. It may not be clear to the modern reader that *cerule* means 'deep blue' or that *ostent* is a sign of something unusual (the *OED* cites Hardy as the only modern user of this otherwise archaic word). The Spirits in *The Dynasts* vary their Saxon phrases with words like *nescience*, *sublunar*, *necessitation*, and such lines as:

Cognizance has marshalled things terrene

and

The free trajection of our entities.

A slightly different problem arises when a common word is used with its Latin meaning rather than one more commonly accepted today. When a man carrying faggots is described as 'so involved in furze that he appeared like a bush on legs' (*RN* 39) we have to take *involved in* of something wound or twisted. Here, as often, the homely and telling simile clashes with the more learned epithet. It was not a habit that Hardy gave up in later years, as the extracts from *The Dynasts* show. In 1891 a critic observed:

Mr. Hardy continually delights in those big Latin and Greek words that seem to be made out of springs rather than vowels.[2]

Greek-based words are less frequent than Latin, but they are often even less common and therefore more intrusive. Sun-worship is called 'the old-time heliolatries' and worship of God *theolatry* (*TD* 102, 292). When Bathsheba gives orders to her workers in the manner of a lawmaker, she is called 'this small thesmothete' (*FFM* 91). When Tess is happy in the sunshine, her hopes mingle with the light to surround her with 'an ideal photosphere' (*TD* 118). The ocean gains alliteration but little else from being called 'the heaving hydrosphere' (*P* 324). Another example of classical lexis appearing awkwardly in an otherwise strong simile occurs in describing Farfrae, a Scot, as possessing 'that hyperborean crispness, stringency and charm, as of a well-braced musical instrument' (*MC* 148). The new art of photography, already bearing a Greek-based name meaning 'light-drawing', need not have been disguised as 'heliographic science' (*AL* 333). There is a particular fondness for adjectives of Greek origin like *autochthonous, diachylon, metamorphic, helical, pachydermatous, trapezoidal*. It is perhaps not surprising that a reviewer of *Tess of the D'Urbervilles* asked 'are the words in *logy* and *ism* necessarily more accurate instruments of thought than simpler phrases?[3]

As well as Latinate and Greek words, Latin phrases are frequently quoted. It must be remembered that these would have been more familiar to Hardy's contemporaries than they are to most modern readers and that classical tags were found in periodicals, sermons and Parliamentary speeches without any sense of affectation. These would be scarcely a sense of departing from normal English usages in phrases like *modus vivendi, pro tem, genius loci, post hoc* argument, *non lucendo* principles. Phrases from modern languages would be almost as familiar to the educated reader, who would accept *soi-disant, lettre-de-cachet, penchant, bizarrerie, éclat* from French and *Weltlust* or *welburgerliche* from German. There was, however, no need to call the open space at the crossroads in the centre of Casterbridge the *carrefour* (*MC* 144, 154).

Sometimes words and phrases which are not rare in themselves and do not aggressively show their classical roots may seem pretentious and unnecessarily formal. Mr Maybold decides to take a letter into the town office 'and obviate the loss of one day in its transmission' (*UG* 185). Angel Clare chooses Tess 'in preference to the other pretty milkmaids when he wished to contemplate contiguous womankind' (*TD* 132). Lucetta's earlier relationship with Henchard 'had been rather the laxity of inadvertence than of intention' (*MC* 229). Fitzpiers, attracted by Grace's pretty face, 'more than wished to annihilate the lineal yard which separated it from his own' (*W* 130).

A show of learning is not confined to classical sources. It was an age when science was becoming both an influence on daily life and a popular hobby for amateurs with leisure to experiment. Hardy was not one of those who set up private laboratories or became expert in some branch of scientific knowledge, but he picked up a good deal of scientific vocabulary and used it in his writing. He could describe the sun falling on a domestic aquarium, 'when the many-coloured zoophytes opened and put forth their arms' (*PBE* 160). The biological word *fibril*, 'thread-like structure', can describe Tess's eyes 'with their radiating fibrils of blue, and black, and gray, and violet' (*TD* 174) and also help to explain the vital principles of the human race, 'fibrils, veins, / Will-tissues, nerves, and pulses of the Cause' (*D* Forescene). Hardy generally manages his scientific terminology effectively and without strain:

> One may say of a look that it is capable of division into as many species, genera, orders, and classes, as the animal world itself. (*HE* 28)

Sometimes the effect depends on more recondite knowledge; we have to know that an *asymptote* is a line which approaches but never reaches a curve in order to appreciate the striking description of the old woman 'to whose earthly course death stood rather as the asymptote than as the end' (*TT* 208). Hardy's neologism *dolorifuge*, on the analogy of *febrifuge* is mannered (*TD* 64). Nor is there much merit in the description of a crowd of men coming with a common purpose 'like the remarkable creatures known as Chain Salpae, which, distinctly organized in other respects, have one will common to a whole family' (*FFM* 85), where the need for explanation makes the simile overtly pedantic.

Words which are comparatively rare may sometimes be very effective in their context, if their oddity is used to emphasise the main point of the sentence rather than for its own sake. This happens when Clare 'again looked into that green trough of sappiness and humidity, the valley of the Var or Froom' (*TD* 173), and when Jude finds Sue 'so uncarnate as to seem at times impossible as a human wife to any man' (*JO* 156). So, too, it seems entirely right for Mrs Yeobright to see 'a painfully well-known figure serpentining upwards by one of the little paths' (*RN* 150), or that Jude in Christminster at night 'serpentined among the shadows' (*JO* 63). The unexpected word is always more acceptable in verse than in prose, and Hardy makes good use of intelligible but unusual words like *bloomage, greenth, frustrance, joyance, tendance*, in his poetry. Objectively, it seems absurd to call an ordinary drinking-glass, a *chalice*, but it comes well in the last stanza of a poem full of nostalgia for a glass long lost under water on a day of love:

> By night, by day, when it shines or lours,
> There lies intact that chalice of ours.   (*P* 337)

Writers have their favourite words which they use often and which become characteristic of their style. We all develop word habits in our conversation and letters, and may even invent words which gain some currency among our close acquaintance. Hardy created the neologism *technicist* to describe an architect doing some of the practical work required by his designs (*AL* 270). He also adopted existing but uncommon words and used them so frequently that he made them distinctively his own. A special favourite was *tremulous*, which he applied specially but not exclusively to a quality of the voice. He may possibly have come to it through Shelley, who also had a liking for it. Characters under the stress of emotion speak 'tremulously' or 'in a tremulous voice', as do John Loveday (*TM* 93), Sue Bridehead (*JO* 81), the Tsar Alexander (*D* 2 I viii) and even the Spirit of the Pities (*D* 3 VII vii). Tess is particularly characterised by this quality, in mood rather than speech; as she grows accustomed to hardship 'she no longer showed any tremulousness' (*TD* 177). Clare finds his life and hers 'tremulous' and she considers that 'There are very few women's lives that are not – tremulous'; Hardy adds, 'pausing over the new word as if it impressed her'. Clare becomes 'tremulous' under strain (*TD* 185, 240). Elfride in one of Hardy's early novels feels 'delight of a tremulous kind' (*PBE* 103), and Sue in his last finds that she and Jude are 'a weak, tremulous pair' (*JO* 241). An old church musician is 'pale and tremulous' (*P* 244), and one of Hardy's best-loved poems, 'Afterwards', begins 'When the Present has latched its postern behind my tremulous stay'.

Another of Hardy's favourite words, less poetic in sound and more obtrusive in use is *rencounter* for an unexpected meeting. Dick Dewy hopes for a rencounter at church with Fancy Day and receives one in passing her cottage (*UG* 62, 87). John and Bob Loveday have one when they see Martha on the stage (*TM* 207) and Ethelberta tries to avoid 'unseemly rencounters' with Lord Mountclere (*HE* 218). Gabriel Oak is 'astonished at the rencounter' when he meets Bathsheba again (*FFM* 64) and Elizabeth-Jane takes a new interest in Lucetta after the rencounter with Farfrae (*MC* 158). 'Rencounters, accidental and contrived' form part of Grace Melbury's marital troubles (*W* 205), Tess is upset by her rencounter with Alec (*TD* 292) and Anny is amused 'by the mere fact of the chance rencounter' with Arabella (*JO* 247). 'A Rencounter' is the title of a section in the story 'The Withered Arm'. The assiduous reader of Hardy comes to greet the word as an old friend, and to give it a certain regard as signalling a meeting within a broken or strained relationship.

Hardy sometimes uses his classical and other literary sources more deeply than in the borrowing of single words. He will make direct reference to a passage which may help in conveying the effect of a person, scene or mood. Such references may appear in either narrative or dialogue; once again it must be remembered that they would have come much more naturally to Hardy's contemporaries than to most of our own. In the early novels the references are sometimes heavy and seem rather forced into the situation, as Manston values his influence with Miss Aldclyffe – 'Like Curius at his Sabine farm, he had counted it his glory not to possess gold himself, but to have power over her who did' (*DR* 191). As Hardy's art develops the classical parallels tend to become briefer and more allusive, as when Farfrae's wife is called 'his Calpurnia' (*MC* 232), with the implication that he is gaining the power of a Caesar in Casterbridge. Myth is used as freely as history; turning the wheel of a grindstone is 'a sort of attenuated variety of Ixion's punishment' (*FFM* 128). The moaning of Tess sounds 'as if it came from a soul bound to some Ixionian wheel' (*TD* 357); old, twisted fruit trees are 'like leafy Laocoons' (*MC* 84); Sue feels a tragic doom over the family like the doom of 'the house of Atreus' (*JO* 239).

Characterisation is often helped by comparison with classical myth or history. Sue in Jude's clothes looks 'boyish as a Ganymedes' (*JO* 128); Angel Clare's idyllic view of Tess is shown when 'he called her Artemis, Demeter, and other fanciful names' (*TD* 141); Dare, asleep, looks like 'an unpedestaled Dionysus' (*AL* 168); Grace is a woman who 'had more of Artemis than of Aphrodite in her constitution' (*W* 279). Aphrodite and her many mythical qualities appears as a linking motif in Pierston's lifelong pursuit in *The Well-Beloved*. Sometimes a single epithet is used to evoke classical associations, as when Alec is aroused by the 'Cyprian image' of Tess (*TD* 293), a couple walk through fog 'like Acherontic shades' (*JO* 306), or the fickle Lucetta displays 'Protean variety' (*MC* 161).

English literature is an even greater source of words and phrases, and one which is likely to be more accessible to the modern reader. It did not play so large a part in formal education as it does today, but those with leisure often read extensively and were able both to use and recognise allusions. Hardy is not alone in this; Victorian novelists often drew on the work of their predecessors, but even so his knowledge is particularly wide and his references are frequent.

Hardy claimed to have started reading Shakespeare when he was twelve, 'for the plots only' (*EL* 31), and during his first years in London he took advantage of the theatre-going which was on offer. He seems to have been particularly moved by a performance of *As You Like It*: one of his earliest poems is addressed 'To an Impersonator of Rosalind' and in 'The Two Rosalinds' he writes of an old woman who once played Rosalind, and indulges in one of his favourite themes as he recalls the lost beauty of youth. There are strong undertones of *King Lear* in *The Mayor of Casterbridge*, and Angel Clare in *Tess of the D'Urbervilles* often quotes Shakespeare and is himself described in terms of Hamlet and other Shakespearean characters.

The literary sources of Hardy's language range over many centuries and genres. As he does with the classical world, he draws on it to help in building up his characters. 'Like Guildenstern, Oak was happy in that he was not over happy' (*FFM* 140). Grace and Marty go to Winterbourne's grave 'like the two mourners in *Cymbeline*' (*W* 295); the perpetrators of the skimmity-ride 'disappeared like the crew of Comus' (*MC* 245); Stephen observes to Knight, 'You out-Hamlet Hamlet in morbidness of mood' (*PBE* 374). The single epithet may be even more telling: Farfrae, in conflict with Henchard and attracted to his daughter, decides 'to enact no Romeo part' (*MC* 115); Viviette's mischievous brother Louis has a 'Puck-like idea' of matchmaking (*TT* 193).

Situations as well as people are referred to literature for heightened effect. Happy children arouse 'The flattering fancy that Heaven lies about them' (*JO* 19); Gabriel, looking down from above at Bathsheba, 'saw her in a birds-eye view, as Milton's

Satan first saw Paradise' (*FFM* 36); Melbury's house is rapidly cleaned, 'as the sweeping of the parlour at the Interpreter's which well-nigh choked the Pilgrim' (*W* 154). Sometimes the allusions are to works more popular a hundred years ago than now. We can respond to Wordsworth, Milton and Bunyan, but may have more difficulty with the way in which shady characters slip out of sight in Mixen Lane and surprise the onlooker 'like Ashton at the disappearance of Ravenswood' (*MC* 225) – a reference to one of Scott's less-known novels, *The Bride of Lammermoor*.

The Bible was familiar to the Victorians, in the Authorised or King James Version. Read aloud in places of worship and privately in the home, its allusions and diction entered into the language as they had done for generations before. Whatever the vagaries of his personal belief, Hardy never lost his love of the Bible. He continued to read it, alluding to it often in letters and personal writing as well as in his fiction and poetry. He would draw on it for many purposes, and his readers would find nothing alien or strained in biblical references extended beyond the overtly religious context.

Characters are displayed with biblical as well as classical and literary analogies. Clym Yeobright 'was a John the Baptist who took ennoblement rather than repentance for his text' (*RN* 171). Henchard visiting the 'conjuror' or white wizard 'felt like Saul at his reception by Samuel' (*MC* 171). Giles Winterbourne keeping the whole truth about divorce law from Grace 'felt like a very Cain' (*W* 260); Jude sitting down by a well thinks 'what a poor Christ he made' (*JO* 102). Swithin 'was as meek as Moses' (*TT* 135); Gabriel Oak, saved from asphyxiation, began 'shaking himself like a Samson' (*FFM* 42).

Situational allusions are also frequent. Knight finds 'it was as hard to be earliest in a woman's heart as it was to be first in the Pool of Bethesda' (*PBE* 329). Gabriel leaves Bathsheba's service 'in placid dignity, as Moses left the presence of Pharaoh' (*FFM* 131); the servant David is removed from household duties 'as peremptorily as Pharaoh's baker' (*TM* 127): Tess and Angel in the early morning feel isolated 'as if they were Adam and Eve' (*TD* 140). Other allusions are more concealed, and for that reason the more effective for the reader who can pick them up. The mingled light and smoke of bonfires is like 'the pillar of a cloud' (*TD* 328): an oak stretches across a lane 'in a manner recalling Absalom's death' (*TT* 74), and conceals a spy who threatens the secret of the lovers. Sir William de Stancy, forced to practise economy, 'raised an altar, as the Athenians did to the unknown God' to this untried virtue (*AL* 291). Father Time seems to be thinking, 'Rightly looked at there is no laughable thing under the sun' (*JO* 233).

The Book of Common Prayer was known as intimately as the Bible, at least to members of the Church of England. A reference to the Thirty-nine Articles aids the brief sketch of the ferry captain who agrees to hold the boat back for Cytherea's brother; 'works of supererogation are the only sacrifices that entice in this way' (*DR* 61). Gabriel Oak's old sheepdog barks at the sheep 'as a sort of Commination service which, though offensive had to be gone through once now and then to frighten the flock for their own good' (*FFM* 46). This Ash Wednesday penitential service is 'blazed forth' in actuality by Torkingham to the discomfiture of Viviette (*TT* 48) and this is only one of many direct references to the Prayer Book as characters in the novels attend services or allude to them.

The use of biblical and prayer-book language by uneducated characters brought some adverse criticism even in Hardy's own time, but other reviewers were prepared to defend him against the charge of inappropriate speech. Even today we may meet people who would lay no claim to learning and are yet able to quote extensively from these sources, and knowledge was certainly greater a few generations ago, when lack of reading skill was compensated by retentive memory for things heard. It was probably not forced, and it is certainly effective, when it is said of a young couple with a well-stocked larder, 'They be for the love and the stalled ox both' with a reference to the Book of Proverbs (*UG* 197). A pert maidservant, seeing the labourers coming for their wages, exclaims 'The Philistines be upon us' (*FFM* 85), and another girl calls *Ecclesiastes* to support her opinion about love that there is 'a time to embrace, and a time to refrain from embracing' (*TD* 152). It seems a little more mannered when Giles says to Grace, 'Your face is like the face of Moses when he came down from the Mount' (*W* 76). The allusion is more natural when Ethelberta's mother-in-law says 'I have been like a Naomi to you in everything' and receives the reply, 'You have been a very good Naomi to me thus far; but Ruth was quite a fast widow in comparison with me' (*HE* 59). The many references made by Jude are completely in character and help to emphasise the irony of his life. The value of any given quotation as used by a particular character has to be decided by the reader's judgement; certainly we cannot imagine Hardy's characters bereft of this area of language.

Direct quotation from another writer, set as an isolated feature of the text, is rather different from allusion or from quotations attributed to characters. It was a practice more acceptable to the Victorian reader, who would enjoy the recognition of the words, and respond to the feeling which had made the author choose them. Even if we now find the practice less natural in a work of fiction, we should not underestimate the importance of that vast corpus of material which we call English Literature in shaping our ideas and the language in which we frame them. It is not only the literary scholar who is influenced, perhaps unconsciously, by this national possession. For the Victorians, as we have seen, familiarity with classical literature was as great or perhaps even greater. The use of another writer's words can be evocative of the context in which they were written and can help to create a similar mood in the new work. They can also give that sense of human continuity through the past to which Hardy was particularly sensitive.

Extended quotation of Hardy's quotations would occupy too much space. Quotations from Greek and Latin authors are generally translated, but sometimes left in the original language. Such quotations are less frequent than the allusions and comparisons which have been noted; they are used several times as epigraphs to sections in *Jude the Obscure*. English literature is quoted a great deal, and not only by characters like Angel Clare. George Somerset is described, in the terms of Dryden's Zimri, as 'Everything by starts and nothing long'. Hardy's favourite, *As You Like It*, helps to express Christopher Julian's feeling about women, 'Come, woo me, woo me; for I am like enough to consent' (*HE* 62). Sometimes Hardy even abandons his own considerable skill of description and lets another writer do the job for him; thus he calls on Chatterton to complete the autumn picture which he has begun, and follows the statement, 'The time was early autumn' with four lines from a song in *Cella* (*W* 164). Often the quotation is shorter and less intrusive; a brief nod to Keats evokes 'the weariness, the fever, and the fret' of London (*PBE* 47); a jocular glance at Tennyson allows Hardy to call the sweat on the faces of country dancers 'a ghastly dew' (*UG* 72). Biblical quotations are similarly sometimes given at length and sometimes briefly. 'Let not your heart be troubled, neither let it be afraid' is congenial to Angel Clare – 'but his heart was troubled all the same' (*TD* 252). When Oak has lost hope of marrying Bathsheba, his thoughts turn to the Bible:

> Gabriel at this time of his life had outgrown the instinctive dislike which every Christian boy has for reading the Bible, perusing it now quite frequently, and he inwardly said, 'I find more bitter than death the woman whose heart is snares and nets'. (*FFM* 144)

Often a short phrase is quoted, perhaps in a context which is ironical rather than devout. There are few writers in English whose language equals that of Hardy for Biblical echoes: 'the one ewe-lamb of pleasure left to him'; 'they walked so circumspectly'; 'tempted unto seventy times seven'; 'voices that had not learnt Creation's groan'; 'turning again to his wallowing in the mire'. Sometimes indeed the words are taken most appropriately, as when the death of Nelson is reported in a moving reference to *Revelation*, 'He has homed to where/ There's no more sea'(*D* 1 V iv).

One of Hardy's great strengths is the range of his vocabulary; one of his weaknesses is his love for words which may be too recondite for the situation in which they are used. He is liable to mix his allusions, a choice which is like the mixed metaphor in weakening both elements and drawing attention to the contrivance of language:

> 'Farewell, thou art too dear for my possessing' had been lengthily discoursed upon that morning by the Coryphaeus of popular opinion; and the spirit having been once poured out sons and daughters could prophesy. (*HE* 134)

This means that a portrait, named after the first line of one of Shakespeare's sonnets, had been discussed in the morning papers and that everyone now felt able to give an opinion on it. The reference to the chorus-leader in Greek drama goes uneasily with the words from *Joel* and a simple statement becomes pretentious and out of proportion to its place in the story.

Although Hardy is too often guilty of this kind of mis-judgement, the overall impression of his work is of English used with all the richness of its great lexis. In both prose and verse he can draw on more areas of language than most of his contemporaries. It has rightly been said of him, 'one feels that with Hardy almost any word could turn up at any moment'.[4] He can arouse our expectations with an unusual word and then send them crashing into bathos, especially under the constraint of metre and rhyme:

> Once engrossing Bridge of Lodi,
> Is thy claim to glory gone?
> Must I pipe a palinody,
> Or be silent thereupon?   (*P* 109)

> Within these hulls, like sheep a-pen,
> Are packed in thousands fighting-men
> And colonels in command.   (*D* 2 III v)

The best of Hardy, and it would be true of many English writers, is found when he turns from the richness of allusion to the simplicity which the language offers equally with its complexity:

> Here is the ancient floor,
> Footworn and hollowed and thin
> Here was the former door
> Where the dead feet walked in,

> She sat here in her chair,
> Smiling into the fire;
> He who played stood there,
> Bowing it higher and higher.   (*P* 166)

Here there is not a word out of place, not a word remote from daily communication. The same is true of the closing words of *Tess of the D'Urbervilles*:

The two speechless gazers bent themselves down to the earth, as if in prayer, and remained thus a long time, absolutely motionless: the flag continued to wave silently. As soon as they had strength they arose, joined hands again, and went on.

This comes immediately after the classical reference to 'the President of the Immortals, in Aeschylean phrase', which has stirred readers to compassion and sometimes to indignation. The learned language is imaginative and powerful, but it is the last two sentences of the book that remain in the mind.

5 Language of Experience

Individual choice of words from the available lexis is partly conditioned by education and reading. Hardy's writing shows that he drew a great deal from these sources of what Giles Winterbourne in *The Woodlanders* calls 'a dictionary word'. The working vocabulary of daily life derives more from the influences of family relationships, environment and personal interests. These combine with the passive and intellectual elements to create the *idiolect* or personal vocabulary. No two people share exactly the same set of words, although the majority will be common to all native speakers of a language.

Many Victorians shared or surpassed Hardy's knowledge of the Bible and of classical and English literature. There can have been few, perhaps no others, who also had a rural childhood and youth, architectural training, a disappointing and childless marriage, with a deep religious sense which moved towards doubt and a feeling that some impersonal destiny ruled human life. All these things, together with other facets of his personality, gave him a vocabulary which was shared and yet distinctive.

Part of Hardy's greatness as a writer comes from the tension between his basically religious and very compassionate nature and his feeling that no higher power really cared about human suffering. His thinking is elusive, not presented in a formal system, and he did not encourage his readers to find a philosophy in his work or to draw moral lessons from it. 'No harmonious philosophy is attempted in these pages – or in any bygone pages of mine, for that matter', he wrote in the preface to his last volume of poems a few months before his death (*PW* 61). Nearly forty years earlier he had given his general opinion that 'the novels which most conduce to moral profit are likely to be among those written without a moral purpose' (*PW* 118).

With due caution, it is possible to find Hardy coming to postulate a kind of Power or Will which stands above all created things, including human endeavour. It is sometimes almost malevolent, but generally seems to be indifferent, or even ignorant, with regard to the affairs of this world. In *The Dynasts* lesser Spirits embody Pity as well as the Sinister, but bow to the Immanent Will.

Much can be said of Hardy's beliefs and their sources; they develop through his life, and are not entirely consistent at any point. In assessing their effect on his language, it can safely be said that a strong sense of fate pervades his work, a sense which is sometimes similar to that of Greek tragedy, sometimes closer to the conflict between destiny and free choice in Elizabethan and Jacobean drama, and often peculiarly Hardy's own. In the essay on fiction quoted above, he praised the novels which 'impress the reader with the inevitableness of character and environment in working out destiny, whether that destiny be just or unjust, enviable or cruel'. Perhaps the nearest we can come to a summary of Hardy's opinion in his own fiction lies in the reflections of Elizabeth-Jane at the end of *The Mayor of Casterbridge*:

> Her strong sense that neither she nor any human being deserved less than was given, did not blind her to the fact that there were others receiving less who had deserved much more . . . she did not cease to wonder at the persistence of the unforeseen . . . that happiness was but the occasional episode in a general drama of pain.

The lives of Hardy's characters often seem to be ruled by the power of fate or destiny, and these words appear frequently. Gabriel without a position is made noble by 'that indifference to fate which . . . often makes a villain of a man' (*FFM* 56). The negative attitude is shown in Manston 'who took upon himself to resist fate with the vindictive determination of a Theomachist' (*DR* 163). Henchard does not 'consider whether destiny were hard upon him or not' (*MC* 122). Characters often use the language of fate, perhaps with the resignation of country people who say 'in their fatalistic way, "It was to be". There lay the pity of it' (*TD* 89) – Hardy adding a conscious or unconscious echo from *Othello*. Alec D'Urberville can speak lightly of fate, with regard to his luck in buying horses – 'It was my fate, I suppose' (*TD* 69). Creedle is philosophical about the failure of Giles's party – ''twere doomed to be so', (*W* 86) and Farfrae is pious about his election as Mayor - 'it's ourselves that are ruled by the Powers above us!' (*MC* 214). The grim words can have a lighter context: Fray, desiring the bailiff's job, is 'gazing blankly at visions of a high destiny apparently visible to him on Billy Smallbury's smock-frock' (*FFM* 107) and Reuben Dewy believes that 'your pa'son [parson] comes by fate' (*UG* 90).

Related words are used to give the same sense, but with a stronger feeling that all events are entirely random. In a poem entitled 'Hap', written very early in his career, Hardy prefers 'some vengeful god' to the feeling that he is ruled by 'Crass Casualty' or 'purblind Doomsters'. A later poem tells of 'the hap of things' (*P* 367) and the word is used more than once in *The Dynasts*, as for example when a combination of damage and clumsiness in a sea battle 'gave hap the upper hand' (1 III i). In the same work the Spirit of the Years reports that

> The cognizance ye mourn, Life's doom to feel,
> If I report it meetly, comes unmeant,
> Emerging with blind gropes from impercipience
> By listless sequence – luckless, tragic Chance,
> In your more human tongue.   (1 V iv)

Another early poem reflects 'What bond-servants of Chance/ We are all' (*P* 18). At the hiring fair a crowd of labourers are 'waiting upon Chance' (*FFM* 55) and Tess suffers from her 'reckless acquiescence in chance' (*TD* 247). The same random quality is felt in 'the impishness of circumstance' which afflicts Swithin (*TT* 51).

An ascription more traditional in English literature relates destiny to the influence of the stars. When Elizabeth-Jane remains attracted to Farfrae, she does not know 'what her malignant star had done to blast the budding attentions' which she had received from him (*MC* 154), but, as Gabriel's hopes prosper, his 'malignant star was assuredly setting fast' (*FFM* 286). Jude resolves to 'battle with his evil star' but has to acquire his learning through 'years of struggle against malignant stars' (*JO* 58, 257). Even more ominously, Tess tells her small brother that 'the stars are worlds' and that the earth is 'a blighted one', just as there are good and bad apples on the trees (*TD* 50). Time can also take on the role of adverse fate – another idea which Hardy's literature shares with that of the Renaissance. 'Treacherous Time' afflicts Melbury in his later years (*W* 47) and Henchard's wife looks like 'one who deems any thing possible at the hands of Time and Chance except, perhaps, fair play' (*MC* 28). The grim irony of naming Jude's son 'Father Time' is revealed in his suicide and killing of the other children. Hardy reflects that 'Sportsman Time but rears his brood to kill' (*P* 15) and recalls a past vision of his wife

> In the running of Time's far glass
> Her crucified.   (*P* 436)

The sense of fate may move away from the direct words into metaphors which represent the thought more obliquely, and it is here that Hardy's imaginative skill is often most fully shown. The word itself may be treated as personified: 'Fate has given us this stab in the back', Sue laments (*JO* 288). People can suffer 'at the hands of Fate' (*TD* 220) or be touched by 'the finger of fate' (*W* 164). Fate can have a 'masked face' (*P* 715) or can show 'waggery' (*RN* 168); after a moment of sadness, 'never will Fates colder-featured/ Hold sway there again' (*P* 430). In a striking phrase, Elizabeth-Jane is said to have the 'fieldmouse fear of the coulter of destiny' (*MC* 93), and Marty South is doomed to manual labour by 'a cast of the die of destiny' (*W* 29).

Metaphor may dispense entirely with the keywords and speak of people forming 'part of the pattern in the great web of human doings then weaving in both hemispheres' (*W* 39). Plans may be thwarted by 'the ingenious machinery contrived by the Gods for reducing human possibilities of amelioration to a minimum' (*MC* 274): a phrase in which Hardy's love of recondite words rather gets the better of him. More effective is the resolution to

> View Life's lottery with misprision
> And its dice that fling no prize!   (*P* 722)

Aspects of experience normally thought of as morally neutral can be given a sinister tone; after Clare's disastrous wedding-day:

The night which had already swallowed up his happiness, and was now digesting it listlessly; and was ready to swallow up the happiness of a thousand other people with as little disturbance or change of mien. (*TD* 231).

As so often, Hardy is most moving when his language is simple and does not labour the thought which it conveys. When the boy Jude is sitting alone and disappointed at his inability to decipher Greek letters:

Somebody might have come along that way who would have asked him his trouble, and might have cheered him by saying that his notions were further advanced than those of his grammarian. But nobody did come, because nobody does.

(*JO* 21)

The language of fate is given particular application to love and marriage. The general feeling about relationships between men and women is that meetings which lead to passion and perhaps to marriage come about either through blind chance or by the design of some mischievous power. The wrong people seem to get married and real love is fated to remain unfulfilled or to result in shame and probably death. The coming tangle of lovers in *The Woodlanders* is seen as one of 'people with converging destinies' (*W* 58). Tess is 'doomed to be seen and coveted that day by the wrong man, and not by some other man, the right and desired one in all respects', to which Hardy adds the typical comment, 'as nearly as humanity can supply the right and desired' (*TD* 60). Pierston is equally misdirected in his search for his ideal, and the image of a puppet emphasises the random helplessness of desire for love:

He was aware, however, that though it might be now, as heretofore, the Loved who danced before him, it was the Goddess behind her who pulled the string of that Jumping Jill. (*WB* 45)

Although Hardy makes great use of Biblical language and frequently alludes in a general way to 'the gods', he seldom expresses himself directly in the language of orthodox theology.

This is logical: he never lost his affection for the words which he had come to know through years of church attendance, but his personal belief was not contained within the faith of the Christian creed and required a different vocabulary. He was, however, enough of a realist in fiction to let his characters speak in words appropriate to believers. Thus Tess has the recollection of orthodox practice to christen her baby with the proper words of the church service (*TD* 109). The theology of marriage is a frequent topic; the sceptical Sue does not 'regard marriage as a sacrament' (*JO* 139) but Bathsheba's father took it so seriously that he could feel desire for his wife only by removing her wedding ring and forgetting she was 'ticketed as my lawful wife' (*FFM* 74). Grace will marry Fitzpiers only if 'our wedding can be at church' (*W* 161) and later believes that 'I am not bound to him by any divine law, after what he has done' (*W* 273).

As is natural for simple characters, the language of theology is usually vague rather than precise; Henchard reflects, 'Who is such a reprobate as I! And yet it seems that even I be in Somebody's hand!' (*MC* 258) and Grace, saved from the man-trap believes 'there has been an Eye watching over us to-night' (*W* 315). A drunk and sceptical postman asserts that 'Not one Christian in our parish would walk half a mile in a rain like this to know whether the Scripture had concluded him under sin or grace' and prophesies that 'they'll do away wi' God a'mighty altogether before long' (*DR* 339). Hardy's own comments are a little more precise, as when the darkness of the sky and total darkness of the heath 'might have represented a venial beside a mortal sin' (*RN* 70).

The theological controversies on which many Victorians thrived and by which many others were troubled are given their due place. The language of both High and Low Church are used in dialogue and commentary. Angel Clare shocks Mercy Chant by talking of monks and monasteries while she in turn, although she says 'I glory in my Protestantism', worries Angel's father by 'decorating the Communion-table – altar, as I was shocked to hear her call it one day' (*TD* 257, 168). *Jude the Obscure* has a great deal of technical church language, as Jude and Sue change their respective positions. Sue works for a firm of ecclesiastical suppliers whose proprietor is 'a dab at ritual . . . wore a cross and beads round her neck as her only ornament, and knew the Christian Year by heart' (*JO* 77). One of the most searching and ironical moments in Hardy comes after the death of the children, when Sue believes that two clergymen in the street are talking about them but Jude reassures her, 'They are two clergymen of different views, arguing about the eastward position' (*JO* 287). In a lighter vein Cain Ball decides to 'play fair' in the disagreements between the churches, 'so I went to High Church in the morning, and High Chapel in the afternoon' (*FFM* 201).

Hardy was well informed about the principal theological and philosophical issues of his time, but he brought to his mature experience the observation and the wisdom of his early years. The life of the countryside, already changing, was a life that he knew intimately and never ceased to love. The sense of immediacy and reality which he shows in his fiction is heightened by the precise descriptions of country crafts and pursuits. Few readers today could check the accuracy of Henchard's equipment as a hay-trusser, but the force of detail carries conviction:

> At his back he carried by a looped strap a rush basket, from which protruded at one end the crutch of a hay-knife, a wimble for hay-bonds being also visible in the aperture.   (*MC* 27)

So, too, we believe that Elizabeth-Jane had gained her skill in netting 'in childhood by making seines in Newsom's home' (*MC* 194) and that Fitzpiers hears 'the tear of the ripping-tool as it ploughed its way along the sticky parting between the trunk and the rind' (*W* 132). The sense of authenticity, of what Henry James called 'felt life' in the novel, can come to us in language which is not our own but has all the strength of the author's experience behind it. Even if the exact meaning of the words is not certain for us, cider-making becomes a real activity when a man is 'engaged in packing the pomace into horse-hair bags with a rammer' (*DR* 154).

The work of the countryside and its language can give life to characters in unexpected ways. The description of the pig-killing in *Jude the Obscure* takes on a tragic dimension as Jude eventually kills the pig too quickly in pity for its suffering. The contrasting characters of Arabella and Jude are brought out in their words. Arabella speaks in the terms of the butcher's trade – 'There's the sticking-knife – the one with the point. Now whatever you do, don't stick un too deep . . . The meat must be well bled' – while Jude has only the language of ordinary compassion – 'A creature I have fed with my own hands . . . have a little pity on the creature' (*JO* 49f). It helps us to understand what is meant when Lord Mountclere fusses around Ethelberta 'like the head scraper at a pig-killing' (*HE* 184). The drudgery and sadness of Tess's life at Flintcomb Ash is brought out more effectively by the detailed description of the work than by commentary:

> They went on seizing the ears of corn, drawing out the straw, gathering it under their arms, and cutting off the ears with their bill-hooks, nothing sounding in the barn but the swish of the straw and the crunch of the hook. (*TD* 279).

The poem 'Throwing a Tree' begins by describing the two woodcutters as 'two executioners' and proceeds through a detailed and seemingly objective account of the falling to its closing line, 'And two hundred years' steady growth has been ended in less than two hours'.

Hardy was one of the last English writers to come really close to the natural world. For him it was a more authentic life than the life of the town; those who came later might love the countryside but could never be quite free from the background of urban dominance. For Hardy Nature was so much a vital force that it could be personified and almost equated with Destiny or the Immanent Will:

> Niggard Nature's trick of birth
>   Bars, lest she overjoy,
> Renewal of the loved on earth
>   Save with alloy.   (*P* 66)

As Pierston tries to talk casually about household matters with the girl to whom he is attracted, 'Nature was working her plans for the next generation under the cloak of a dialogue on linen' (*WB* 64). 'O why should Nature's law be mutual butchery!' Sue exclaims (*JO* 261) and Giles more resignedly feels the power of destiny in the unchanging natural laws: 'When the sun shines flat on the north front of Sherston Abbey – that's when my happiness will come to me' (*W* 259).

The features of the countryside seem to take on a life of their own, so that their very names are evocative. Flowers are precisely identified; instead of a general description of shapes and colours, we have to see the gardens of Casterbridge through the language of flowers themselves, 'the mossy gardens at the back, glowing with nasturtiums, fuchsias, scarlet geraniums, "bloody warriors", snap-dragons and dahlias' (*MC* 72); so too the Welland gardens:

> The lilac, the laburnum, and the guelder-rose hung out their respective colours of purple, yellow and white; whilst within these, belted round from every disturbing gale, rose the columbine, the peony, the larkspur, and the Solomon's seal. (*TT* 117)

It may be commented, without damage to the effect of the passages, that Hardy was taking liberties in both cases with the time of flowering of some of the specimens. Similar effect is given by the varieties of apples for cider, 'Horner and Cleeves apple for the body, a few Tom Putts for colour, and just a dab of old Five-corners for sparkle' (*TM* 120). Trees dominate *The Woodlanders*, oppressing those to whom they give a way of life:

> The breeze was oozing through the network of boughs as through a strainer; the trunks and larger branches stood against the light of the sky in the forms of sentinels, gigantic candelabra, pikes, halberds, lances, and whatever else the fancy chose to make of them. (*W* 231)

In this novel old South feels that his life is bound up with the tree before his window; when it is felled, he dies. The Romantic sense of a link between human and non-human animate life, which Ruskin dubbed 'the pathetic fallacy' often takes a sad or sinister turn in Hardy. As a woman parts from her lover:

> She heard in the waves as the daytide wore,
> And read in the leer of the sun that shone,
> That they parted for evermore. (*P* 155)

The repetition of a word applicable to both human and inanimate sounds is made with fine effect:

The sea moaned, more than moaned – among the boulders below the ruins, a throe of its tide being timed to regular intervals. These sounds were accompanied by an equally periodic moan from the interior of the cottage chamber.

(*WB* 95f).

But elsewhere Hardy contrasts the heedless natural world with the value-based world of human life. Tess feels that 'a wet day was the expression of unremediable grief at her weakness' but Hardy comments that she had broken a social law, 'but no law known to the environment in which she fancied herself such an anomaly' (*TD* 101)

The beauty of nature can also be loved for itself; some of Hardy's best writing is found in his descriptions of country scenes. He knew the natural world in all its seasons and all its moods, and the reader never goes very far in his work without finding language used with power to create on the page a scene that takes the mind into the region of sensory impressions.' The great description of Egdon Heath which opens *The Return of the Native* is often cited; there are many others, whose full effect needs more extended quotation than is possible here. A less familiar example may illustrate Hardy's skill in the choice and variety of words: a dawn scene over the sea:

A huge inflamed sun was breasting the horizon beyond a sheet of embayed sea which, to her surprise and delight, the mansion overlooked. The brilliant disc fired all the waves that lay between it and the shore at the bottom of the grounds, where the water tossed the ruddy light from one undulation to another in glares as large and clear as mirrors, incessantly altering them, destroying them, and creating them again; while further off they multiplied, thickened, and ran into one another like struggling armies, till they met the fiery source of them all.   (*HE* 29)

Hardy desires to create a sense of the red (and therefore threatening) morning light, made dynamic and animated by its reflection in the water. He uses a wide range of vocabulary for each effect, combined in a single description. The sun is *inflamed, brilliant*, it *fired* the waves with *ruddy light* in *glares* from its *fiery source*.

The light itself is full of movement, *breasting the horizon*, and the water *tossed* the light in *undulation*, with the increasing power of *mirrors . . . altering . . . destroying . . . creating*, while the reflections *multiplied, thickened*. Then the simile 'ran into one another like struggling armies' gives a climax to the single words and leads the description of change back to the static *fiery source* which re-names the *inflamed sun* of the opening sentence, so that movement is brought out of wholeness and at last led back to it.

One of the qualities which make Hardy outstanding as a recorder of the natural world is the precision with which he observes it. In the poem 'Afterwards' he writes of some of the minutiae of country sights and sounds, wondering whether after his death people will say 'He was a man who used to notice such things'. He chooses words so precisely that there is a danger of their seeming mannered and forced, a danger from which he nearly always escapes by the sense of personal knowledge which comes through. Thus a human pulse feels to a shepherd like 'the same quick, hard beat in the femoral artery of his lambs when overdriven' (*FFM* 66), and an exhausted woman breathes 'like a lamb when you drive him till he's nearly done for' (*RN* 265). Hardy notices how the early morning rays of the sun 'made every shallow dip in the ground to show as a well-marked hollow' (*PBE* 131) and how at dusk 'the little birds in the hedges were rustling their feathers and tucking themselves in comfortably for the night' (*FFM* 58). He can take us through the year without naming a single month or season by moving from the spring when 'The sparrow dips in his wheel-rut bath' to winter when 'Icicles tag the church-aisle leads' (*P* 493f); he pities the fashionable woman who has never seen

> The way a robin will skip and come,
> With an eye half bold, half timorsome,
> To the table's edge for a breakfast crumb.   (*P* 767)

He brings the reader into a later summer morning 'when the grass is never dry in the shade' simply by naming and describing the little details which converge into the whole:

> Fuchsias and dahlias were laden until eleven o'clock with small drops and dashes of water, changing the colour of their

sparkle at every movement of the air; and elsewhere hanging on twigs like small silver fruit. The threads of garden-spiders appeared thick and polished. In the dry and sunny places dozens of long-legged crane-flies whizzed off the grass at every step the passer took. (*UG* 142)

The natural eye of the countryman was, in Hardy, sharpened by training as an architect. Reference has already been made to the way in which a speaker who is an architect is given verisimilitude by his use of technical terms, but the language of architecture is not confined to the several characters in the novels who practise that profession. It is natural that a medieval mason who is the supposed voice of a poem should know of *archmould, tracery, ogees* and *cusping-marks* ('The Abbey Mason'); but Hardy also uses language from this area of knowledge when he is the detached narrator of a story. He describes buildings with the same precision of detail as he uses for natural scenes, and with the same effect of cumulative persuasion. Hintock House has 'grey lead roofs . . . with their gutters, laps, rolls and skylights' and 'Elizabethan windows, mullioned and hooded, worked in rich snuff-coloured freestone' (*W* 69). An old church has a 'chevroned doorway' (*AL* 37); another house has 'three gables and a cross roof behind . . . mullioned and transomed windows' (*DR* 133); yet another has 'the hooded windows, simple string-courses and random masonry of the Gothic workman' combined with the later addition of the classical 'equal-spaced ashlar, architraves and fasciae' (*HE* 229). Jude, as a skilled stonemason, can recognise an *ogee dome, mullioned and transomed windows* and *corbel-heads*; it is Hardy himself who sees a city in a valley below, 'its more prominent buildings showing as in an isometric drawing' (*TD* 372).

The humbler buildings of the countryfolk who are his principal characters receive no less loving and detailed observation. Tranter Dewy lives in 'a long low cottage with a hipped roof of thatch, having dormer windows breaking up into the eaves' (*UG* 37); Overcombe Mill also has 'hips instead of gables' (*TM* 34); we may need to go to a dictionary to discover that a hipped roof slopes at the ends down to the eaves, where a gabled one has a triangular section of wall rising to the summit, but the named detail adequately creates the simple structure and prepares us for the type of people who are living in it. The description of the great barn on Bathsheba's farm is a brilliant passage, in which the nobility of the ancient building, and its importance to the rural community, is shown by extended comparisons with the architecture of a church. It has its *transepts, porches, heavy-pointed arches, striding buttresses* and *lancet openings* and a roof 'far nobler in design . . . than those in nine-tenths of our modern churches' (*FFM* 137f).

The language of architecture is allowed to extend as metaphor beyond the description of buildings. In *Jude the Obscure*, Gothic architecture represents the ancient faith which Hardy believes to have had its day. Jude, through his years of believing, works in the Gothic style, although the sceptical Sue thinks that 'Gothic is barbaric art' and prefers the railway station to the cathedral as a symbol of modern life (*JO* 259, 112). The argument between classical and medieval is strong throughout *A Laodicean* and again relates to the nature of leading characters.[1] People can have architectural characteristics as well as opinions. Lucetta arranges her body on a couch 'in the cyma-recta curve which so became her' (*MC* 147) and Eustacia's lips form 'the curve so well known in the art of design as the cima-recta or ogee' (*RN* 82; the difference in spelling is Hardy's).

Hardy learned architecture as a profession; he came to love painting as a personal pleasure. During his early residence in London he visited many galleries and exhibitions, and began to keep a notebook about artists and schools. It was an interest which remained with him all his life and extended to modern as well as classical art. In 1889 he found the 'pictures of the year . . . not very great', but liked the exhibition of Monet – 'you could almost feel the heat of the sun depicted in the painting' (*CL* I 191). He was at the Tissot exhibition ten years later and planning to go to the Summer Exhibition at the Royal Academy in 1900 (*CL* II 234, 255). His response to Monet is typical: he loved the sensory feeling which painting can evoke and which he himself could create with equal force through the use of language.

Allusions in Hardy's work to painters and painting ranges very widely. Rembrandt was a particular favourite and we read of the 'Rembrandt effects' of the diffused sunlight inside a tent

(*FFM* 296). 'Rembrandt's intensest manner' focuses attention on a single person (*RN* 140), and another character looks like 'a highlight portrait by Vandyck or Rembrandt' (*AL* 141). More obscure painters are also evoked, and here the lack of familiarity is liable to make the verbal reference seem more strained and less effective. Cows are seen in a field which is 'speckled as thickly with them as a canvas by Van Alsloot or Sallaert with burghers' (*TD* 117), and the complexion of a country girl has 'the softened ruddiness on a surface of high rotundity that we meet with in a Terburg or a Gerald Douw' (*FFM* 82). In his own century, Hardy had a special regard for Turner, especially the later paintings. He found his taste moving away from naturalism and noted in 1887 that 'the much decried, mad, late-Turner rendering is now necessary to create my interest' (*EL* 243). Earlier he had observed the garish gaslights on butchers' stalls making 'splotches of orange and vermilion, like the wild colouring of Turner's later pictures' (*PBE* 164) and seeing the grey coat of an old dog changed to reddish brown, 'as if the blue component of the grey had faded, like the indigo from the same kind of colour in Turner's pictures' (*FFM* 52).

The influence of visual art on a writer is obviously of a different nature from that of literature. While literature comes as language, inviting direct quotation and helping by transference to shape the personal idiolect, painting has nothing to offer linguistically except the technical language standing at one remove from it in art criticism. The writer must use the existing resources of language to transmit his own experience of a picture and to make that experience help the imagined world which he is creating through language. Hardy often describes his characters by analogies with painting. Some examples have been quoted; another amusing if slightly forced comparison shows Ethelberta 'in a dress sloped about as high over the shoulder as would have drawn approval from Reynolds, and expostulation from Lely' (*HE* 231).

More evocative is the description of the old woman who had 'the mellow hue of an old sketch in oils – notably some of Nicholas Poussin's' (*FFM* 144). The appeal to a painter for support of a highly vivid verbal description is particularly effective in poetry. Hardy, as so often, remembers former beauty now lost in age and wonders:

Do I know these, slack-shaped and wan,
Whose substance, one time fresh and furrowless,
Is now a rag drawn over a skeleton,
As in El Greco's canvases? (*P* 702)

Faces especially suggest the resemblances to portraits. Elizabeth-Jane has bright eyes 'as if Nature had been advised by Correggio in their creation' (*MC* 108). Jude's aged aunt has 'a countenance like that of Sebastiano's Lazarus', and Jude himself in distress resembles a statue, with 'lines about his mouth like those in the Laocoön' (*JO* 159, 103). The profile of Avice is 'not unlike that of one of the three goddesses in Rubens's "Judgement of Paris",' (*WB* 67) and Bathsheba is likened not to a portrait but to part of a landscape when her face 'coloured with the angry crimson of a Danby sunset' (*FFM* 130).

Landscapes and other scenes are often mentioned to describe the settings against which the characters live. The countryside after rain is as bright as 'the landscapes by Ruysdael and Hobbema' (*FFM* 275). A clean tablecloth is 'reticulated with folds as in Flemish Last-Suppers' (*W* 82).

The pictorial language is often made most effective when the scene is 'framed' in a window or other opening. The description of sunrise in *The Hand of Ethelberta* quoted above is seen when a blind is drawn up on a window. Cytherea sees her father fall to his death as she looks through a window and watches the spire like 'an illuminated miniature, framed in by the dark margin of the window, the keen-edged shadiness of which emphasized by contrast the softness of the objects enclosed' (*DR* 46). Somerset sees Dare 'in a square of darkness formed by one of the open windows' (*AL* 141), and Percomb watches Marty through a window (*W* 28), while Lucetta and Elizabeth-Jane see the market place and the brightly-painted new agricultural machine as they look from inside a room (*MC* 155). Hardy gave *Under the Greenwood Tree* the sub-title, 'A Rural Painting of the Dutch School'. His sense of form and colour is strong and does not always need the support of direct allusion to pictures. Tess walks with her family as she parts from them, with a child at each hand and her mother behind, 'the group forming a picture of honest beauty flanked by innocence, and backed by simple-souled vanity' (*TD* 67). Some of the most memorable scenes in the novels are strongly visual in composition: the knacker's farm which Ethelberta and Picotee visit: the building of the bonfire on Rainbarrow; the different breeds of sheep converging on Greenhill Fair. Often a single phrase works strongly on the eye of imagination. A load of hay passes a window and 'a yellow flood of reflected sunlight filled the room for a few instants' (*MC* 163); two lovers stroll 'aqua-tinted by the weak moon and mist' (*TM* 200); the sun penetrates the morning haze and 'broke through chinks of cottage shutters, throwing stripes like red-hot pokers upon cupboards, chests of drawers, and other furniture within' (*TD* 102).

Another way in which Hardy draws on his experience is in his creation of place names. The region of 'Wessex' is precisely mapped and events are located in towns and villages which, for devoted readers, have taken on a reality of their own and almost replaced their originals. Transformations may be simple, as when Weymouth becomes *Budmouth*, Bournemouth *Sandbourne*, Corfe Castle *Corvesgate Castle*, and Lulworth Cove *Lulwind Cove*. Sometimes Latin forms produce the new name and make Winchester into *Wintoncester* or Shaftesbury into *Shaston*, or the Latin form may be translated and made *Kingsbere* from Bere Regis. The new name is sometimes allusive: *Quartershot* embodies the military barracks of Aldershot and *Christminster* refers to the college and cathedral of Christ Church at Oxford. Others are invented and have come to be associated closely with certain novels, like *Mellstock* for the hamlets around Hardy's birthplace, *Casterbridge* for Dorchester and the sinister-sounding *Marlott* for the home of Tess.

Real names are sometimes retained and can be evocative as when changing human responses to nature seem to foreshadow a time when 'Heidelberg and Baden be passed unheeded' by the traveller as he 'hastens from the Alps to the sand-dunes of Scheveningen' (*RN* 32). Real and invented names combine to suggest the hardships of a homeless life in 'A Trampwoman's Tragedy':

> Through the Great Forest, Blackmoor wide,
>   And where the Parret ran.
> We'd faced the gusts on Mendip ridge,
> Had crossed the Yeo unhelped by bridge,
> Been stung by every Marshwood midge,
>   I and my fancy-man.

A cumulative, almost Miltonic, effect is gained by a catalogue
of names which, mostly unknown to modern readers, suggest the
devastating reality of the Napoleonic campaigns:

> And Kollowrath – now on the Pratzen heights –
> Will down and cross the Goldbach rivulet,
> Seize Tilnitz, Kobelnitz, and hamlets nigh,
> Turn the French right, move onwards in their rear,
> Cross Schwarsa, hold the great Vienna road.   (*D* 1 VI iii)

Hardy's personal names are equally inventive and often
striking. Place names may be given to people, as Jude is
named after the village Fawley, which itself becomes *Marygreen*,
and Gillingham gives its name to Philotson's friend and is trans-
formed into *Leddenton*. *Chickerel*, *Hinton*, *Melbury*, *Petherwin*
and *Winterbourne* are family names derived from place names in
the area of the novels. Some names are 'right' in their suggestion
of the qualities of the bearer; such are *Oak*, *William Worm*,
Joseph Poorgrass. Others are in the English literary tradition of
names which more directly embody vocations or characteristics;
The Hand of Ethelberta has a horse-knacker called *Neigh*, an antiquarian *Dr Yore*, an organist *Dr Breeve* and builders called *Messrs
Nockett and Perch*. A bishop who signs 'Timothy Titus Philemon'
(*TM* 151) is perhaps rather heavy humour; there is more subtlety
in the barber *Percomb* of *The Woodlanders*, with its suggestion
of 'peruke' and 'comb'. Forenames are often Biblical, a realistic
derivation from the prevailing country custom of the time, giving
Bathsheba, *Gabriel*, *Jude* and *Solomon* among others. Women
sometimes have more fanciful names, which perhaps are meant to
go with their affected and indecisive characters: such are *Elfride*,
Ethelberta, *Eustacia*, *Lucetta* and *Viviette*. There is irony in the
naming of the idealistic but unfortunate *Angel Clare*, and a moving
sense of nostalgia for home as well as physical distance in the Scot
Farfrae. All these, however, were more fortunate than *Cain Ball*,
whose 'mother made a mistake at his christening, thinking 'twas
Abel killed Cain' (*FFM* 89).

6   The Pattern of Words

A writer's freedom to select from the lexis of the language is constrained by the rules of grammar on how words may be placed and combined. English allows a good deal of latitude in the association of words, although there is a basic word order which cannot be ignored. The language of literature takes particular advantage of this latitude, and some writers have pushed it to the limit of communication. Hardy was not so adventurous as his contemporary, Gerard Manley Hopkins, whose poetry is full of long and daring compounds and unusual collocations; and he came nowhere near James Joyce in this century, whose later work is written in what is almost a new language. Hardy did, however, show skill and invention in the manipulation of words. The great range of his literary vocabulary gave him material to experiment with usage and to let his imagination work in many directions.

Some writers have enriched the vocabulary of English by coining new words which have passed into regular use. Among many such *neologisms* we have *blatant* from Spenser and *pandemonium* from Milton. Although exaggerated claims have been made for Hardy's original contributions to the language, he was not a great creator of entirely new words. His adaptations of existing words are often striking in context but have not been found to supply a lasting need; among them are *technicist, reverberances* and *fantocine* ('puppet'). As will be seen later, he made much use of dialect and helped to preserve in a literary corpus many Dorset words which were already disappearing from living speech. His great strength lies in his power of combining words in unexpected ways, either in their normal grammatical relationships or by the creation of new compounds.

A simple but effective use of words is the listing of a number of items related to the same object or experience, a device well known in traditional rhetoric by the name *enumeratio*. The cumulative effect of the words gives strength to the basic item with which they are semantically connected and brings it into prominence for the reader. It is not necessary to be able to identify each item accurately; the conviction of reality is imaginative rather than intellectual. It may be for creatures of the natural world, like 'the pet cocks and hens . . . Hamburghs, Bantams, Cochins, Brahmas, Dorkings, and such other sorts as were in fashion just then' (*TD* 74). The effect may be as strong in a list of artefacts; we believe in the existence of the local volunteers who are 'duly equipped with pouches, cross-belts, firelocks, flint-boxes, pickers, worms, magazines, priming-horns, heel-ball, and pomatum' (*TM* 186), even though we probably need notes to tell us what most of these things are. A similar list is woven into metre and rhyme in the poem 'The Alarm', with a sudden and moving change of reference in the last line:

> Now, to turn to marching matters:
> I've my knapsack, firelock, spatters,
> Crossbelts, priming-horn, stock, bay'net, blackball, clay,
> Pouch, magazine, and flint-box that at every quick-step
> clatters:
> My heart, Dear; that must stay!

The art of *enumeratio* can be used to bring out the author's own concealed comment. There is quiet irony in Sue Bridehead, the sceptic, being employed in a shop which 'contained Anglican books, stationery, texts and fancy goods: little plaster angels on brackets, Gothic-framed pictures of saints, ebony crosses that were almost crucifixes, prayer-books that were almost missals' (*JO* 71). It can be extended until the idea takes on a life of its own and becomes almost an additional character in the story. As Henchard's wife and her daughter come into Casterbridge for the first time, we see through their eyes the nature of the town which is to shape their destiny:

> The agricultural and pastoral character of the people upon whom the town depended for its existence was shown by the class of objects displayed in the shop windows. Scythes, reap-hooks, sheep-shears, bill-hooks, spades, mattocks, and

hoes at the ironmonger's; bee-hives, butter-firkins, churns, milking stools and pails, hay-rakes, field-flagons, and seed-lips at the cooper's; cart-ropes and plough-harness at the saddler's; carts, wheel-barrows, and mill-gear at the wheel-wright's and machinists's; horse-embrocations at the chemist's; at the glover's and leather-cutters, hedging-gloves, thatchers' knee-caps, ploughmen's leggings, villagers' pattens and clogs.

(*MC* 48)

These are lists of words sharing the same part of speech. The combination of words related grammatically is the regular basis of language and can be imaginatively used to good effect. The use of many adjectives is often condemned as poor style, showing a weakness in vocabulary and dependence on a few nouns qualified by their different attributes. While there is truth in this, it is also true that the careful choice of adjectives can be highly effective and make the general become particular in a striking way. Adjectives need be neither banal nor merely objectively informative. Hardy often surprises the reader by his adjectival phrases, which can say in a pair of words as much as a long piece of description. People are described by their appearance or actions; we begin to understand Arabella as a threat to Jude when she speaks with 'a jealous, tigerish indrawing of breath' (*JO* 41) and Mrs Garland's social position is summed up as a 'twilight rank' (*TM* 55). Melbury's confidence in Fitzpiers is replaced by a 'feline stealth' (*W* 199); Viviette acts with 'unvarnished simplicity' (*TT* 47); a remembered girl has an 'aspen form' and speaks 'with spectral frail alarm' (*P* 839). The adjectives may be combined in a phrase that adds narrative change to basic quality, as when Izz Huett is called a 'good-natured and now tippling girl' (*TD* 265). Faces have an endless fascination for Hardy. Sometimes, as we have seen, he compares them to figures in paintings, but often a single word is enough: 'peachy cheeks', 'two sapphirine eyes', 'holmberry lips'.

Natural scenes and the movements of the countryside also follow Hardy's minute observation. The vagaries of the weather, more apparent than in towns, are succinctly expressed as 'clammy breeze', 'spectral, half-compounded, aqueous light'; 'icicled drops'. Sometimes observation shows the intimate knowledge which few, even in his own time, would have shared: bonfires made from heath and furze burn with a 'clear, kingly effulgence', straw and beanstalks give only 'rapid flares and extinctions', but harder woods endure with 'steady unaltering eyes' (*RN* 50). Perhaps the architect's eye looks at natural scenes and sees a 'segmental hill' (*TT* 2); at other times the adjective may be more conventionally literary and describe a 'pellucid stream' (*JO* 31) or Hardy may lapse into his fondness for recondite words and describe the winter light as 'achromatic chaos' (*TD* 277).

His natural observation and his love of the visual work together to give a strong sense of colour to his adjectival choices. This is not an uncommon skill in a writer; what makes Hardy's phrases more interesting is his attachment of colour words to objects and even abstractions not usually thought of in this way. He can write of a 'green smile', 'red wrath', 'silvery singings', 'a diaphanous slice of bread'. Words other than colour ones can be applied in this manner: an abstract noun is associated with both feeling and sound: 'the freezing negative that those scholared walls had echoed to his desire' (*JO* 283). Emotions can be described as 'lively and sparkling', a church as 'grizzled' (*MC* 285, 48). The effect is not of the startling deviance from normal usage practised by some later writers, but rather the evocation of qualities which seem appropriate once they have been discerned through these connections of words.

Adjectives can be still more originally paired with nouns, so that the words seem to contradict one another in the figure known as *oxymoron*. The effect is of a momentary pause in acceptance, followed by understanding of a truth to be extracted from the point of rest between opposing qualities. Such combinations are used to describe the unsettled nature of Eustacia:

> Her appearance accorded well with this smouldering rebellious-
> ness, and the shady splendour of her beauty was the real surface
> of the sad and stifled warmth within her.   (*RN* 82)

The phrase *smouldering rebelliousness* is a fairly conventional metaphor, but the following vision of splendour which is *shady* and warmth which is *sad and stifled* reverses expectation and prepares the reader for contradictions within the character; similarly, but more succinctly, the mixed-up Sue Bridehead is said to possess 'epicene tenderness' and to have 'closed her lips in retortive silence' (*JO* 127, 158). Crickett, the parish clerk, is tellingly described as a 'Bowdlerized rake' (*DR* 155) with reference to Thomas Bowdler's expurgated edition of Shakespeare for 'family reading'. The natural world can show similar contradictions, as at dusk 'the dubious daylight ended' (*P* 199).

Hardy frequently uses nouns in the position, and with the function, of adjectives. Lucetta's house in Casterbridge has an 'ashlar front' (*MC* 180); *ashlar*, a block of dressed and squared stone, is a favourite word with Hardy the former architect. A man newly in love is 'in the aspen stage of attachment, and open to agitation at the merest trifles' ('The Distracted Preacher'). Honour is given to 'sage Milton's wormwood words' (*P* 106). Proper nouns are particularly effective when used in this way, usually given adjectival suffixes for the purpose.

Hardy's resources of classical, biblical and literary knowledge are drawn upon: Jude writes a letter with 'Rhadamanthine strictness' (*JO* 305); a huntsman is 'panting with Actaeonic excitement' (*W* 92) and Fitzpiers has 'a fit of Achillean moodiness' (*W* 182); Troy wears 'a heavy grey overcoat of Noachian cut' (*FFM* 315); Angel Clare is 'less Byronic than Shelleyan (*TD* 194). A more topical allusion appears when we read of 'a town young man, with a Tussaud complexion and well-pencilled brows half-way up his forehead' (*HE* 21).

Hardy's greatest originality, however, is shown in his creation of compound words, and it is here that he may be said to have enriched the literary vocabulary of English most remarkably. The formation of new words by combining two or more existing words is one of the basic methods in English, a facility going back to the Old English of Anglo-Saxon times and one which is shared with other languages of the Germanic family. Hardy learned something from William Barnes, who tried to avoid Romance words by combining Saxon ones to give the same meaning, and who used many novel compounds in his poetry. Hardy defended Barnes's practice, calling his coinages 'singularly precise and beautiful definitions of what is signified' (*PW* 71).

The same praise could be given to Hardy's own best work in this mode of invention. Sometimes the compounds themselves are not strikingly original but are successful because of the sensitive placing. Thus Elizabeth-Jane is 'a dumb, deep-feeling, great-eyed creature' (*MC* 128); a woman in a poem is 'haughty-hearted'; the poetic speaker 'paused amid the laugh-loud feast' (*P* 828, 913).

Other combinations are notable in themselves, with imaginative power reinforced by their context. Adjectives formed by combination with past participles are characteristic of Hardy. Gabriel sees Bathsheba 'in the cold morning light of open-shuttered disillusion' (*FFM* 130); a church is 'many-chevroned' (*RN* 179). Hardy's poetry is very rich in compounds of this type: a small selection offers 'dim-discerned train', 'tall-spired town', 'new-vamped abbey', 'wind-thridded suit', 'large-pupilled vision', 'foam-fingered sea', 'neutral-tinted haps'.

A combination of two nouns is the most common type of this formation in English, giving familiar words like *railway, steamship, teaspoon.* Hardy combines nouns in this way, sometimes using the result as an adjective as when Flintcomb-Ash is called a 'starve-acre place' (*TD* 273). A more traditional type of noun-compound is used when the configurations of the ground are seen as 'the very finger-touches of the last geological change' (*RN* 34). Troy describes Bathsheba as his 'Juno-wife' (*FFM* 313). Other combinations are created, following the flexibility of English in this respect; a noun and adjective combine to make an adverb when a girl 'passed foot-faint with averted head' (*P* 626). Longer compounds are also used, and here Hardy passes beyond the normal expectations of the daily language into conscious but effective literary invention with phrases like 'the All-Earth-gladdening law/ Of Peace (*P* 90) and the 'sword-and-pistol air' which Festus Derriman affects (*TM* 172).

Some of Hardy's inventions have an effect close to that of the 'kenning' used in Old English poetry, in which a pair of words stands as a descriptive substitute for a more familiar single item: thus the sea is called the 'whale's-road' or a feather a 'bird's-joy'. Hardy can describe the trees and hedges as 'summer's green wonder-work', sorrow as 'heart-bane', female ancestors as 'foredames', the contact of dancing as 'tightening arm-embowments', a glance as an 'eye-sweep'. To these from the range of non-dramatic poetry may be added two examples from *The Dynasts*: Napoleon considers that events may pause 'for a wink-while'; the Chorus prepares to move 'as we were swallow-vanned'.

Hardy shows equal facility in the coining of words by the process of *derivation*: adding prefixes or suffixes to extend the meanings of basic words. This aspect of English word-formation, although not unknown in Old English, owes more to the Romance element and is the dominant method in modern languages descended from Latin. Hardy is fond of prefixes like *up-*, *out-*, *over-*, *in-*, *en-*; he has a fine power of transforming familiar words by the apparently trivial addition. A particular favourite of his is 'embrowned', which he applies as a verb to Egdon Heath, as a participial adjective to dead leaves and in the form 'embrowning' to the twilight. He emphasises its melancholy tone by repetition when he writes how the past has faded for him:

> Its gentle echoes faintlier played
>   At eves upon my ear
> Than when the autumn's look embrowned
>   The lonely chambers here,
> When autumn's settling shades embrowned
>   Nooks that it haunted near.   (*P* 308)

Other coinages from the poetry are many, and range across the regular parts of speech. Some examples are: 'bedrenches', 'outfigure', 'enghosted', 'enringed', 'beglimpsed', 'entroughed', 'enjailed'.

Without overstating the hackneyed theme of Hardy's pessimism, we may find some significance in the frequency of words derived by the prefixing of the negative *un–* particle. The beautiful and moving poem 'Tess's Lament' has:

> I cannot bear my fate as writ,
>   I'd have my life unbe,

where the short disyllable *unbe* combines one of the most common English prefixes with one of the most common verbs to convey utter despair and weariness.[1] Longer formations, one of them oddly used as a participle, create the mood of lonely death:

> One there in pain reclining,
>   Unpardoned, unadieu'd   (*P* 450)

The negative prefix is repeated with a dulling sense of resignation:

> Not God nor Demon can undo the done,
> Unsight the seen,
> Make muted music be as unbegun.   (*P* 310)

Other such coinages include 'unhelped', 'unhope', 'unmine', 'unconscienced', 'unvision', 'unclocked', 'unforeknowingly'. The negative sense is conveyed also through the suffix *-less*:

> Led by sheer senselessness
> And presciencelessness
> Into unreason   (*P* 836)

and coinages like 'checkless', 'serviceless'.

An interesting device which Hardy may have learned from Barnes is the creation of a single word from phrasal verbs. A verb followed by a preposition is common in English, especially in colloquial usage; it is a form of the splitting of words which together form a single meaning, which is called *tmesis*. Hardy likes to convert tmesis into a compound word, to strengthen the sense by avoiding separation and throwing emphasis on the verb as the stressed syllable:

> The clock rang;
> The hour brought a hand to deliver;
> I upsprang,
> And look back at den, ditch and river,
> And sang.   (*P* 523)

Similar force is given to unexpected phrases like 'night ondrew', 'I am so overgloomed', 'we . . . downlooking stood', 'the sun had upswum'. A further movement creates a noun from the reversal and combination of verb and preposition: 'in its overblow', 'eyes in their quick, keen upthrow'.

Another type of deviation from common usage is practised by many writers; it breaks no rules of formation or placing, but selects a word or phrase which would normally seem odd or inappropriate at that place in the sequence. When Phillotson begins to hope for future happiness it is said that he 'lived with a forward eye' (*JO* 304). Not a word in the phrase is 'against the rules', yet it momentarily startles the reader. A man may have an eye to the future, or live in hope, or take a forward look: it is the suggestion of more than one idiom, and the completion of none, which makes the combination effective. A woman who thinks she is being teased neither pouts nor looks affronted but 'looked a pout' (*WB* 41). A pillow-case is made from 'an old surplice which had been excommunicated the previous Easter' (*HE* 274): an amusingly suitable word but not one which most of us would think of applying to a worn-out garment. A mingling of verbal economy with audacity of choice makes such phrases prominent and forces attention on the actions which they describe.

The traditional grammar of English, based on Latin tradition, assigns each word in the language to one of eight 'parts of speech'. It is a system which works well enough with most words for a simple analysis, but soon proves inadequate. The word *round* can, in current usage, be a noun, verb, adjective, adverb or preposition. A word is readily given a new function if the process helps communication: in recent years words traditionally categorised as nouns have been used as verbs, including *contact, service, loan* and *officer*. Purists may object, but the process of transference has been going on for centuries, and no one now thinks it odd to use *walk* or *adult* as nouns, though the first was originally a verb and the second an adjective. Hardy often takes transference farther than normal usage and in so doing draws on the vitality of English without loss of communication. The effect and associations of a word can be heightened by putting it into an unusual grammatical relationship with its context.

Nouns are used as verbs, particularly in the poems. Hardy has 'I pilgrimed', 'a hardship to be calendared', 'we stood psalming', 'an aura zephyring round', 'where my friend had lectioned the prophets'. A strong, pitiful effect is achieved by the statement, 'Henchard stood as if idiotized' (*MC* 189) and there is deep pathos in the single deviant word when the Chaplain speaks as Nelson dies, 'He has homed to where/ There's no more sea' (*D* 1 V iv). A proper name is boldly used to create one of the pictorial effects which Hardy loves:

The previously gilded but now dreary hills began to lose their daylight aspects of rotundity, and to become black discs vandyked against the sky. (*PBE* 392)

A verb may be used as a noun: when a young woman sings to her lover, 'her warble flung its woo/In his ear' and a baby is provoked to give 'cries of annoy' (*P* 564, 739). Other types of words are also given nominal function; the long history of the Roman road makes 'thoughtful men/Contrast its days of Now and Then' (*P* 264).

Hardy is especially fond of using adjectives as verbs, a change which brings a qualitative sense into the action without the need for an additional adverb. Sometimes little is gained except the convenience of metre as when *darked* is used instead of darkened in 'he *darked* my cottage door' (*P* 268), and 'will dark our door' (*P* 268, 619). Something more than economy of syllables is achieved in the line, 'Loves who have falsed their vows' (*P* 630). The use of *wan* as a verb has precedent in Shakespeare,[2] but Hardy makes it his own with:

The eyes that beamed out rapid brightness
  Have longtime found their close,
The cheeks have wanned to whiteness
That used to sort with summer rose

and 'The blurred lamps wanning her face' (*P* 830, 455). Hardy's sense of early mortality finds perfect expression in the line, 'ears that have greened but will never be gold' (*P* 942). The fading sound of a ghostly song is described – 'It smalled, and died away' – and the same transference is used to tell how the vision of a dead woman passes back through time into nothingness, 'and smiled till she was nought at all' (*P* 259, 529).

In all these ways, Hardy takes various liberties with words but applies them in the sense which they generally convey: *green* still refers to colour, *small* to size or quantity and so on. Literary usage stretches the resources of language still further by figurative use, in which words refer to something that is suggested by association with their common meaning, but not related to it in a literal sense. Figurative language is, of course, not confined to literature; we are all accustomed to stock comparisons like 'as good as gold', 'as merry as a cricket', and metaphors which refer to 'the light of experience', 'the heat of the moment'. In fact, much more of our language is metaphorical than we commonly realise. There is no conscious metaphor today in speaking of the *foot* of a hill or the *hands* of a watch, since these are the only words normally available for the required meaning. We have to probe very deeply into the history of the language to learn that *ponder* is really a figurative use of a word meaning 'to weigh' and that *dependent* originally had the sense of hanging from something. The difference in literary usage is that figurative language is more frequent and more imaginative, directed to the effect desired at that point in the text.

The simplest form of figure is the direct comparison or *simile*, successful if it transfers the quality of experience into the world of imagination. It may be a brief statement that one thing is like another, or may be extended into a longer analogy which creates a picture of its own and exerts the writer's power of description as well as his gift of comparison. Hardy uses both types, though his analogies are usually succinct and not taken to the length practised by writers as different as Dickens and Virginia Woolf. He uses similes to describe characters, the natural world, human artefacts and even abstract qualities – all of them important aspects of his work. A detailed study would occupy a whole book in itself and a selection must suggest the fertility of his invention.

Hardy's country people live very close to nature, and he often described them in terms of the natural world. It is perhaps not highly imaginative to see a connection between milkmaids and their charges: 'all the girls drew onward to the spot where the cows were grazing in the farther mead, the bevy advancing with the bold grace of wild animals' (*TD* 177). There is more power in the reaction of the women to the killing of Troy: 'all the female guests were huddled aghast against the walls like sheep in a storm' (*FFM* 326) or in Grace Melbury with Mrs Charmond, 'like a wild animal on first confronting a mirror or other puzzling product of civilization' (*W* 216).

The rural analogy may be extended into the town, as Ethelberta confronts an audience of 'rows of listeners showing themselves like a drilled-in crop of which not a seed has failed' (*HE* 83). Elfride in the London docks is 'like a rainbow in a murky sky' (*PBE* 307). Shakespeare is seen in homely terms:

Like a strange bright bird we sometimes find
To mingle with the barn-door brood awhile,
Then vanish from their homely domicile. (*P* 440)

The comparisons can be incongruous, even grotesque, yet make
their effect strongly. When Lucetta is overcome by distress, she
sits with 'her limbs hanging like flails' (*MC* 180). Mrs Swancourt
hastens to seek shelter from the rain, 'waddling . . . like a hard-
driven duck' (*PBE* 192). Tess stands in the open country 'like a
fly on a billiard-table of indefinite length, and of no more consequence to the surroundings than that fly' (*TD* 119). A publican
has 'a globular stomach and small legs, resembling a top on two
pegs' (*JO* 245). The architect's eye sees a man 'standing as still
as a caryatid' (*AL* 229), and a deceived husband 'stood as stiff as
a caryatid' (*P* 370).

A simile is used with tragic irony in *Jude the Obscure*; when
Arabella plans the seduction which is the beginning of Jude's
decline, she falls to the ground and 'lay supine, and straight as
an arrow'; at the end of the book Jude lies dead, 'covered with
a sheet, and straight as an arrow' (*JO* 39, 346).

Faces, which always fascinate Hardy, attract a variety of comparisons. The young Jude smiles:

With that singularly beautiful irradiation which is seen to spread
on young faces at the inception of some glorious idea, as if a
supernatural lamp were held inside their transparent natures.

(*JO* 19).

When Gabriel Oak smiles, wrinkles appear round his eyes,
'extending upon his countenance like the rays in a rudimentary
sketch of the rising sun' (*FFM* 27). The less agreeable smile of
Festus Derriman shows his teeth 'like snow in a Dutch cabbage'
(*TM* 51). More sombrely, Sue sees the marriage licence and 'her
look was that of the condemned criminal who catches sight of
his coffin' (*JO* 310). A daughter's features can be seen in her
father's face 'as the landscape is in the map, the romance in the
history, the aim in the deed' (*HE* 283). Ugly and disagreeable
faces draw almost Dickensian images, like the anonymous man
who has 'a nose 'resembling a copper knob, a damp voice, and
eyes like button-holes' (*MC* 33) or Lord Mountclere whose eyes
'gleamed like a couple of tarnished buttons' (*HE* 310). Another

old man is seen 'opening and shutting his mouth quite silently like a thirsty frog, which was his way of expressing mirth' (*TM* 63) and Gabriel Oak 'stared sternly at the one lengthy and two round faces . . . which confronted him with the expressions of a fiddle and a couple of warming-pans' (*FFM* 252).

Individual features are often picked out in this way. Cainy Ball runs in, 'his mouth red and open, like the bell of a penny trumpet' (*FFM* 127); an old man has a single tooth, 'which made much of itself by standing prominent, like a milestone in a bank' (*FFM* 68). A maidservant's eyes dilate 'like circles in a pond' (*UG* 97) and eyebrows are arched so that they look like 'two slurs in music' (*UG* 71), while half-closed eyes become 'little straight lines like hyphens' (*UG* 72). A sailor's scarred face has 'a jagged streak like the geological remains of a lobster' (*TM* 265).

Actions as well as features are made vivid by analogy, again often taken from nature. Eustacia hesitates about whether she could pursue Clym and 'haunt the environs of his mother's house like a robin' (*RN* 126) and Dare slips away from the scene of his mischief 'as unostentatiously as a cat that has upset the family china' (*AL* 332). Boldwood picks up the unconscious Bathsheba 'as a child might have taken a storm-beaten bird and arranged its ruffled plumes' (*FFM* 283); Fancy follows Dick, 'trotting after him like a pet lamb' (*UG* 146). Other activities are set firmly in the human world: Elizabeth-Jane is prepared for a shock, 'as the box passenger foresees the approaching jerk from some channel across the highway' (*MC* 115); Tess, arriving at Alec's house, 'stood hesitating like a bather about to make his plunge' (*TD* 57), and Gabriel Oak is snubbed by the bailiff passing him 'as a Christian edges past an offertory-plate when he does not mean to contribute' (*FFM* 64).

As people are seen in terms of nature, the natural world takes analogies from outside itself. Animals may suggest the inanimate: a bull has nostrils 'like the Thames Tunnel as seen in the perspective toys of yore' (*MC* 185); a flock of sheep form a pattern 'not unlike a vandyked lace collar, to which the clump of furze-bushes stood in the position of a weaver's neck' (*FFM* 217); gulls 'glint out like silver flecks' (*P* 494). Trees drop dead boughs 'like ichthyosauri in a museum' and have 'jackets of lichen and stockings of moss' (*W* 276). A curl of smoke from a chimney is 'like a blue feather in a lady's hat' (*UG* 110); a whole landscape can lose its animation:

A clamminess hangs over all like a clout,
The fields are a water-colour washed out,
The sky at its rim leaves a chink of light,
Like the lid of a pot that will not close tight. (*P* 391)

Even the sun can become ugly and sinister 'like a great inflamed wound in the sky' (*TD* 144) or 'like a red and flameless fire shining over a white hearthstone' (*FFM* 104).

The weather, vital in the fortunes of those who live by the land, is shown in many moods. The sunset can be peaceful and promising on 'the evening of a fine spring day . . . its outline being lost in cloudy masses hanging round it like wild locks of hair' (*UG* 88). More often the weather seems to be stormy and inimical to the characters:

> Sometimes a bough from an adjoining tree was swayed so low as to smite the roof in the manner of a gigantic hand smiting the mouth of an adversary, to be followed by a trickle of rain, as blood from the wound. (*W* 274).

The wind may throw raindrops 'like peas against the panes' (*RN* 324), and a sundial is given a voice to say:

> I drip, drip here
> In Atlantic rain,
> Falling like handfuls
> Of Winnowed grain,
> Which, tear-like, down
> My gnomon drain. (*P* 808)

When heavy rain destroys the flowers on the grave of Fanny Robins, the simile used is bizarre and matches the other wild incongruities that have accompanied her death: 'the rich tawny mould was stirred into motion, and boiled like chocolate' (*FFM* 274). A softer rain greets Susan Henchard's second wedding with sad heaviness:

> It was a windless morning of warm November rain, which floated down like meal, and lay in a powdery form on the nap of hats and coats. (*MC* 90).

Raindrops on a gate hang 'like silver buttons ranged in a row' (*P* 480), and comparison with another human artefact captures the hot damp of a stormy summer: 'it rubbed people's faces like a damp flannel when they walked abroad' (*MC* 173).

Artefacts can themselves have likenesses, which may give them a sense of animation. A high-backed settle is, 'to the hearths of old-fashioned cavernous fireplaces, what the east belt of trees is to the exposed country estate, or the north wall to the garden' (*RN* 140). Lamps on a sea-wall send 'long tap-roots of fire quivering down deep into the sea' (*DR* 82). Hardy's sense of the continuity of time creates the image of cups in a tavern 'forming a ring round the margin of the great sixteen-legged oak table, like the monolithic circle at Stonehenge in its pristine days' (*MC* 205). An old man's crinkled writing is 'like the coastline of Tierra del Fuego' (*HE* 224). A large sun-hat inspires a detailed analogy with 'a brim like a wheel whose spokes were radiating folds of muslin lining the brim, a black margin beyond the muslin being the felloe' (*WB* 106). These are light and pleasant images but a tragic foreshadowing is given when Tess speaks of souls leaving bodies during life and Crick looks at her with 'his great knife and fork . . . planted erect on the table, like the beginning of a gallows' (*TD* 132).

Human moods are made concrete through imagery; detailed analysis of feelings can be dispensed with when a single analogy communicates to the reader. When Clym Yeobright sees his dying mother, 'distress came over him like cold air from a cave' (*RN* 270), and the scandal of Lucetta's letters to Henchard 'was spreading like a miasmatic fog' (*MC* 233). After Clym's love for Eustacia, any later love 'would be a plant of slow and laboured growth, and in the end only small and sickly, like an autumn-hatched bird' (*RN* 348), and 'the vows of man and maid are frail as flimsy gossamers' (*P* 230). A savagely dynamic image describes how Tess 'dismissed the past – trod upon it and put it out, as one treads on a coal that is smouldering and dangerous' (*TD* 193). Less tormented by the past, Elfride 'could slough off a sadness and replace it by a hope as easily as a lizard renews a diseased limb' (*PBE* 166). The hard nature of Manston is expressed by the way his true feelings 'remained locked within him as in a casket of steel' (*DR* 190). Reality and fancy mingle in the bewilderment of Melbury in a series of analogies:

The scene to him was not the material environment of his person, but a tragic vision that travelled with him like an envelope. Through this vision the incidents of the moment but gleamed confusedly here and there, as an outer landscape through the high-coloured scenes of a stained window. (*W* 210)

A lighter irony compares the impact of Swinburne's poems on the age of Victoria:

It was as though a garland of red roses
Had fallen about the hood of some snug nun. (*P* 323)

An interesting aspect of Hardy's use of simile is his acute awareness of the contemporary world as well as the timeless world of nature and human history. If his great characters have an almost archetypal quality, the language that describes them and their environment reveals them to be men and women of the nineteenth century. The Christminster dons pass 'across the field of Jude's vision like inaccessible planets across an object glass' (*JO* 279). The popular 'magic lantern' gives the picture of clouds which 'hastened on in a body, as if painted on a moving slide' (*RN* 201) and of a weary feeling that God is made in man's fancy:

One thin as a phasm on a lantern-slide
Shown forth in the dark upon some dim sheet,
And by none but its showman vivified. (*P* 325)

Troy manipulates his sword 'as quick as electricity' and in comparison with him 'Oak had a melancholy tendency to look like a candle beside gas' (*FFM* 170, 216). The rural world can take on the images of the encroaching towns, with the saps 'Beginning to heave with the force of hydraulic lifts inside all the trunks of the forest' (*W* 223); and the same force creates 'bustlings, strainings, united thrusts, and pulls-all-together, in comparison with which the powerful tugs of cranes and pulleys in a noisy city are but pigmy efforts' (*FFM* 120). A grim simile of a menace which was dreaded in town and country alike compares Oak's statement to prospective employers that he had had his own farm to 'a rumour of cholera' (*FFM* 57).

Hardy makes more extensive use of simile, simple or developed, than of the more concise figure of *metaphor* which leaps over the bridge of overt comparison and expresses one referent in direct terms of another. He does, however, use metaphor to show human qualities. Clym's eyes have 'an icy shine' (*RN* 296); Farfrae is 'quite brimming with sentiment' (*MC* 153); Alec is 'the blood-red ray in the spectrum' of Tess's life (*TD* 59); Paula's uncle is 'a breathing refrigerator' (*AL* 274). Other metaphors for people include 'a willing tool', 'netted lion', 'the obscurest cellarage of his brain', 'reed in council, rock in fire'. The modern world appears when Lord Mountclere's mouth twitches as 'the telegraph needles of a hundred little arctic messages from his heart to his brain' (*HE* 252), and when Swancourt has to 'act the part of a fly-wheel towards the somewhat irregular forces of his visitor' (*PBE* 59). Relationships give metaphorical language: a greeting is an 'elixir', drinkers are 'limed and caught by the ensnaring inn', a bonnet and shawl are 'pitchforked on in a moment'. Arabella is determined to remarry and 'wind Jude up to the striking-point' (*JO* 323); a rural image enlivens a town gathering when Pierston moves across a crowded room 'using the toes of his dress-boots as coulters with which he ploughed his way' (*WB* 44).

The natural world also has its metaphors, sometimes commonplace like 'the silver face of the moon' or trees 'antlered with dead branches', but sometimes striking as when Christminster is 'at the northernmost point of the crinkled line along which the leisurely Thames strokes the fields of the ancient kingdom' of Wessex (*JO* 62) or carved figures are 'cloaked with little cobwebs' (*AL* 405). Human and natural light are juxtaposed in metaphor as a door opens and 'a golden rod of light would stripe the ground for a moment and vanish again, leaving nothing outside but the glowworm shine of the pale lamp amid the evergreens over the door' (*FFM* 316). The animate and the inanimate come together when a bundle of clothes is unwrapped and 'a baby appeared as the kernel to the husks' (*RN* 326) and when it is observed that 'man, even to himself, is a palimpsest, having an ostensible writing, and another beneath the lines' (*FFM* 218).

These are only a few of Hardy's figurative manipulations of language. The range and imagination of his analogies is astonishing and is a major part of his literary genius. His use of imagery is a quality which has been called Shakespearean, and the epithet is not exaggerated. Some of his contemporaries were overwhelmed by the richness; one critic resorted to his own analogy in commenting:

> His similes and metaphors are often strained and far-fetched, and his style gives one the idea of a literary gymnast who is always striving after sensation in the form of some *tour de force*.[3]

The modern reader must make an individual judgement, based on the total effect of these figures through a text rather than on scattered examples. Some may feel that his power to make words convey a meaning beyond their normal reference puts Hardy among the greatest masters of the English language.

7 Syntax and Structure

Hardy has often been adversely criticised for clumsiness in the structure of his sentences. The attacks of some critics give the impression of an almost illiterate writer struggling with little success to control the complexities of the English sentence. He himself recognised that 'a sentence may often be strictly correct in grammar, but wretched in style' (*CL* IV 89). It is easy to point out weaknesses in his style and foolish to pretend that they do not exist. The discerning reader accepts that Hardy's writing is uneven but prefers to give most attention to its many positive qualities. As with his vocabulary, his handling of syntax can sometimes be awkward but is more often successful.

A tendency to very long sentences is more frequent in Victorian style than in recent writing. Hardy sometimes gets a great deal into one sentence; he and his contemporaries had grounding in the Latin periodic sentence as well as the natural flexibility of English. A sentence can extend to a paragraph of fifteen lines of print (*TT* 167), with the aid of conjunctions and semi-colons joining main clauses which could grammatically be written as separate sentences. A slightly shorter example shows the method:

> In their sad doubts as to whether their son had himself any right whatever to the title he claimed for the unknown young woman, Mr. and Mrs. Clare began to feel it as an advantage not to be overlooked that she at least was sound in her views; especially as the conjunction of the pair must have arisen by an act of Providence; for Angel never would have made orthodoxy a condition of his choice.   (*TD* 169)

This is clear enough, even if it seems too long for modern taste. There are times when Hardy's sentences run less smoothly:

94

Such silent proceedings as those of this evening were repeated
many and oft times when he was not under the eye of the
boys, whose quick and penetrating regard would frequently
become almost intolerable to the self-conscious master in his
present anxious care for Sue, making him, in the grey hours
of morning, dread to meet anew the gimlet glances, lest they
should read what the dream within him was. (*JO* 135)

This is given a jerky effect by the passive verbs at the beginning, qualified by a relative clause of time with a prepositional
phrase which is then immediately followed by an adjectival clause.
The pronominal subject *he* becomes a noun-phrase, *self-conscious
master*, in the middle of the sentence. The subordinate noun *regard*
becomes the subject of the main verb *become* and governs the
participle *making*. There is nothing wrong in any of these choices,
but the combination of them obscures and reduces the main thrust
of the sentence. The effect is made worse by the heavy *repeated
many and oft times* followed by *frequently* and the weak ending
on the copula *was* which makes the sentence trail away.

The example illustrates several of Hardy's recurring faults in
sentence structure. Weak endings sometimes follow subordinate
openings which collapse into a brief and uninspiring statement of
the main clause:

However, after these words of self-depreciation, which were
let fall as much for her own future ease of conscience as for
his present warning, she made no more ado. (*HE* 234)

Excessive relative clauses and sub-clauses are a source of trouble;
a sentence starts to amble on through relative pronouns and linking
participles as if uncertain of its destination:

He also, from time to time, slipped sweet shy glances at her
profile; noticing the set of her head, the curve of her throat,
and other artistic properties of the lively goddess, who the while
kept up a rather free, not to say too free, conversation with Mr.
Shiner sitting opposite; which, after some uneasy criticism, and
much shifting of argument backwards and forwards in Dick's
mind, he decided not to consider of alarming significance.
(*UG* 78)

> The two or three arches of these vaults that were still in position had been utilized by the adjoining farmer as shelter for his calves, the floor being spread with straw, amid which the young creatures rustled, cooling their thirsty tongues by licking the quaint Norman carving, which glistened with the moisture. (*W* 154)

This is the debit side of Hardy's structure; he can also be strikingly brief and simple. He has the great virtue of careful balance in a paragraph, going from the short one-clause statement to the longer complex sentence of exposition and back to simplicity:

> Clare could bear this no longer. His eyes were full of tears, which seemed like drops of molten lead. He bade a quick good-night to these sincere and simple souls whom he loved so well; who knew neither the world, the flesh, nor the devil in their own hearts; only as something vague and external to themselves. He went to his own chamber. (*TD* 255)

This is clear in expression and varied in rhythm: controlled variation is one of the hallmarks of good prose. A succession of short sentences, with enough variety of construction to avoid banality, can be wonderfully effective:

> The oblique band of sunlight which followed her through the door became the young wife well. It illuminated her as her presence illuminated the heath. In her movements, in her gaze, she reminded the beholder of a feathered creature who lived around her home. All similes and allegories concerning her began and ended with birds. There was as much variety in her motions as in their flight. (*RN* 203)

Despite occasional misfortunes with runaway sentences, Hardy's control is usually strong and assured. He has a fine sense of balance within the sentence as well as in the development of a paragraph; it has been suggested that this may be a legacy of his architectural training.[1] The training in classical rhetoric which was part of education in his early years perhaps also helped, and there is also the fact that his prose is the prose of a poet. Antithesis of structure can combine with prose rhythm to give sentences which are artistically pleasing and fall in strong cadence:

> Their position was perhaps the happiest of all positions in the social scale, being above the line at which neediness ends, and below the line at which the *convenances* begin to cramp natural feeling, and the stress of threadbare modishness makes too little of enough. (*TD* 139)

> The laboured resistance which Lady Constantine's judgement had offered to her rebellious affection ere she learnt that she was a widow, now passed into a bashfulness that rendered her almost as unstable of mood as before. (*TT* 69)

Parallel structures and semantic opposites are used to good effect, especially in building up a character:

> If an emotion possessed him at all, it ruled him; a feeling not mastering him was entirely latent. Stagnant or rapid, it was never slow. He was always hit mortally, or he was missed. (*FFM* 119)

> She had planned many things and fulfilled few. (*HE* 157)

> People who began by beholding him ended by perusing him.
> (*RN* 141)

A person, scene or event may be described by a statement of opposite and a negative emphasis which builds up a positive effect:

> He was in the agricultural world, but not of it. He served fire and smoke; these denizens of the fields served vegetable, water, frost and sun. (*TD* 309)

Double negatives are dangerous things in English and can lead to the vague flabbiness characteristic of much official jargon, but they can also be used to produce a striking affirmation:

> There was no part of Paula's journey in which Somerset did not think of her. (*AL* 281)

A single negative with the antonymn of the intended meaning can have a similarly strong effect:

These shaggy recesses were at all seasons a familiar surrounding to Olly and Mrs. Yeobright; and the addition of darkness lends no frightfulness to the face of a friend.   (*RN* 56)

Negative understatement is another means of emphasis:

The dress of their sister for today was exactly that of a respectable workman's relative who had no particular ambition in the matter of fashion – a black stuff gown, a plain bonnet to match.   (*HE* 134)

Another way in which Hardy gives strength to his sentences is the cumulative effect of enumeration in individual items. The majesty of the great woods is emphasised by a sentence which moves from the ground to fallen leaves, the lower parts of trees and then to their heights:

They went noiselessly over mats of starry moss, rustled through interspersed tracts of leaves, skirted trunks with spreading roots whose mossed rinds made them like hands wearing green gloves; elbowed old elms and ashes with great forks, in which stood pools of water that overflowed on rainy days and ran down their stems in green cascades.   (*W* 64)

The force of the nouns is increased by the use of verbs suggesting increasingly difficult progress: *went, rustled, skirted, elbowed*. A weary journey can also be described by the device of moving downwards in the hierarchy of roads:

The turnpike-road became a lane, the lane a cart-track, the cart-track a bridle-path, the bridle-path a foot-way, the foot-way overgrown.   (*MC* 170)

Hardy often achieves a strong effect by the use of syntax; he is fond of concessional clauses and can use them to affirm his point by seeming to move away from it before making it the main statement of the sentence. Thus Jude at first persuades himself that his attraction to Sue is spiritual; the concession towards his own self-deception breaks into assertion of the reality:

> Though he was loth to suspect it, some people might have said to him that the atmosphere blew as distinctly from Cyprus as from Galilee. . . . For though it had seemed to him to have an ecclesiastical bias during the service, and he had persuaded himself that such was the case, he could not altogether be blind to the real nature of the magnetism. (*JO* 75)

The character can be shown as more conscious of the tension:

> Though exhibiting indifference, Somerset had felt a pang of disappointment when he heard the news of Paula's approaching dinner-party. (*AL* 127)

or the tension can be in the place of action:

> Though the upper part of Durnover was mainly composed of a curious congeries of barns and farmsteads, there was a less picturesque side to the parish. (*MC* 223)

There is a good example of cumulative contrast and concession in the climactic scene when Tess and Angel reach Stonehenge; the uncertainty and menaces, what Hardy might have called the 'tremulous' quality of the situation, is brought out:

> Though the sky was dense with cloud a diffused light from some fragment of a moon had hitherto helped them a little. But the moon had now sunk, the clouds seemed to settle almost on their heads, and the night grew as dark as a cave. However, they found their way along, keeping as much on the turf as possible that their tread might not resound. (*TD* 368)

Other types of subordinate openings are frequent. They sometimes weaken the sentence, but often strengthen it by leading up to the main clause and giving it final emphasis. Infinitive opening construction can have this effect:

> To add to the difficulty he could gain no sound of the sailor's name. (*MC* 39)

> To be left to pass the evening by herself was irksome to her at any time, and this evening it was more irksome than usual by reason of the excitement of the past hours. (*RN* 274)

Present or past participles can be used similarly:

> Perceiving that they had really pained her, they said no more, and order again prevailed. (*TD* 36)

> Turning off the gas, and slamming together the door, they went downstairs and into the street. (*PBE* 165)

> Influenced by a second thought she readily obeyed. (*TD* 218)

> Occupied thus, with eyes stretched afar, Oak gradually perceived that what he had previously taken to be a star low down behind the outskirts of the plantation was in reality no such thing. (*FFM* 35)

Subordinate clauses placed at the beginning of a sentence also have a rhetorically cumulative effect. Clauses of time can be effective in passing from the temporal setting to the human focus:

> One night, at the end of August, when Bathsheba's experiences as a married woman were still new, and when the weather was yet dry and sultry, a man stood motionless in the stackyard of Weatherbury Upper Farm, looking at the moon and sky.
> (*FFM* 214)

> When she turned from her interested gaze at this scene, there stood John Loveday. (*TM* 101)

An opening noun-clause gives a strong initial emphasis, leading in turn to still further weight when the main clause is reached. The construction may seem less idiomatic to the modern reader, who may prefer a different form ('It is unlikely that he will come', rather than 'That he will come is unlikely') but it is sound nineteenth-century syntax and Hardy uses its potential:

> That Eustacia was somehow the cause of Wildeve's carelessness in relation to the marriage had at once been Venn's conclusion on hearing of the secret meeting between them. (*RN* 94)

> That the clothes he had borrowed were some cast-off garments of the late Sir Blount had occured to St. Cleeve in taking them. (*TT* 109)

> That she looked up at and adored her new lover from below his pedestal, was even more perceptible than that she had smiled down at Stephen from a height above him. (*PBE* 269)

There is a particularly fine example in the poem 'The Impercipient' which opens with a sequence of noun-clauses combining as the subject of the simple last line in the stanza:

> That with this bright believing band
>   I have no claim to be,
> That faiths by which my comrades stand
>   Seem fantasies to me,
> And mirage-mists their Shining Land,
>   Is a strange destiny.

In his enthusiasm for subordinate openings, Hardy is sometimes guilty of the unrelated or 'hanging' participle: the understood subject of the participle is different from that of the main verb. This is counted an offence against formal grammar, but in practice seldom leads to misunderstanding. It is doubtful if the reader who is not making a close textual study will be confused or affronted by a sentence like:

Having caught ear of Melbury's intelligence while she had stood on the landing at his house, and been eased of much of her mental distress, her sense of personal decorum had returned upon her with a rush.   (*W* 237)

Some such sentences, however, may become clumsy; and once attention is drawn to the structure the desired effect is lost. A combination of participles in different relationships with passive verbs lacking a firm subject makes this sentence fall apart:

Going up, the floors above were found to have a very irregular surface, rising to ridges, sinking into valleys; and being just then uncarpeted, the face of the boards was seen to be eaten into innumerable vermiculations.   (*FFM* 82)

The collapse is made complete by the heavily formal *vermiculations* at the end. A less catastrophic, but still potentially ludicrous, effect is made when Hardy writes:

Looking over the damp sod in the direction of the sun a glistening ripple of gossamer webs was visible to the eye under the luminary, like the tack of moonlight on the sea.   (*TD* 200)

While we are castigating Hardy for offences against grammar, it must be admitted that he is sometimes guilty of the split infinitive: a source of fury to some purists, but a fault which many writers commit and which does not always seem unidiomatic:

It would have demanded the poetic passion of some joyous Elizabethan lyrist like Lodge, Nashe, or Greene to fitly phrase Paula's presentation of herself at this moment.   (*AL* 197)

He was no longer disposed to stick at trifles in his investigation, and did not hesitate to gently open the front door without ringing.   (*W* 226)

Such minor lapses are less interesting than Hardy's capacity for turning potential weakness to strength. In general, the English sentence needs to rest upon the verb for its effect; a mass of nouns supported by a single verb of general meaning can easily become weak or be lost in abstraction. In a paragraph which tells of the continuing traces of Roman occupation in Casterbridge, Hardy describes how 'some tall soldier or other of the Empire' was frequently unearthed in digging fields and gardens. The anonymous skeleton becomes real, a silent actor in the drama, in a sentence which begins by making it the transferred subject of a passive verb, works through a series of noun-phrases dependent on the opening clause and culminates in an active verb whose subject is people in the living present:

> He was mostly found lying on his side, in an oval scoop in the chalk, like a chicken in its shell; his knees drawn up to his chest; sometimes with the remains of his spear against his arm; a fibula or brooch of bronze on his breast or forehead; an urn at his knees, a jar at his throat, a bottle at his mouth; and mystified conjecture pouring down upon him from the eyes of Casterbridge street boys and men, who had turned a moment to gaze at the familiar spectacle as they passed by. (*MC* 79)

Another good use of nominal construction is deictic presentation: a noun is made particular and prominent in the context by the definite article or a demonstrative. We see Tess, at the opening of a chapter, going wearily on her way after her seduction:

> The basket was heavy and the bundle was large, but she lugged them along like a person who did not find her especial burden in material things. (*TD* 92)

The *basket* and *bundle*, not previously described, take on a power of their own in the particularity with which they begin the sentence and the inner sorrow is emphasised when this power yields to the negativity of all *material things*. Deixis may point back to a previous sentence and draw attention to an item which had seemed unimportant on its first mention. The reference may be to the same noun; Henchard 'indulged in an occasional loud laugh at some remark among the guests' and the surface warmth of the statement is chilled by the stark opening of the next sentence:

> That laugh was not encouraging to strangers; and hence it may have been well that it was rarely heard.   (*MC* 51)

The backward reference may be more oblique, with a verbal statement focused sharply in a succeeding noun. Eustacia with the villagers at the festival 'looked among them in vain for the cattle-dealer's wife who had suggested that she should come', and the negative action becomes a positive situation:

> This unexpected absence of the only local resident whom Eustacia knew considerably damaged her scheme for an afternoon of reckless gaiety.   (*RN* 243)

The deixis may have no antecedent but may emphasise the general truth of a statement, offered with a demonstrative force that assumes the reader's agreement:

> That touching faith in members of long-established families as such, irrespective of their personal condition or character, which is still found among old-fashioned people in the rural districts, reached its full perfection in Melbury.   (*W* 152)

Another means of emphasis is inversion of normal word order. English syntax in general requires fairly rigid adherence to a conventional order of words in a sentence, as pointers to their grammatical function. With no inflexions to distinguish cases of nouns, it can normally be assumed that a noun is the subject of a verb which it precedes and the object of a transitive verb which it immediately follows. Departures from expectation have a strong effect when they can be made without ambiguity or distortion of meaning. We are all familiar with remarks like 'Down came the rain' or 'this I cannot understand'. Hardy has a good control of permissible inversion. An adverb at the beginning of a sentence makes a dynamic start and prepares for the verb thus directed:

> Down, downward they went, and yet further down – their descent at each step seeming to outmeasure their advance.
>
> (*RN* 56)

Indoors they went. Did he want any tea? No, it was too late: he would rather sit and talk to her. (*JO* 42)

The placing of a verb before its auxiliary in a statement gives prominence to the action or state, particularly when it is negative:

Elfride loved him, he knew, and he could not leave off loving her; but marry her he would not. (*PBE* 364)

Before putting out the light he re-read Tess's impassioned letter. Sleep, however, he could not. (*TD* 354)

The object of a sentence may gain priority of importance over the subject by inversion:

Her social hardships she could conceal. (*TD* 282)

All these things he gazed upon. (*TM* 226)

A separation of phrases normally written in sequence gives a strong ending:

To the coarse materiality of that rivalry it added an inflaming soul. (*MC* 167)

Inversion is accepted in poetry, often as a device to aid the regularity of the verse rather than for emphasis, though the two may be combined. Hardy takes advantage of the convention, usually with moderation:

Though fervent was our vow,
Though ruddily ran our pleasure   (*P* 227)

The first of many to enthrall
My spirit, will it be?   (*P* 433)

Enough. As yet disquiet clings
About us. Rest shall we.   (*P* 68)

Sometimes the syntax becomes distorted enough to detract from the strength of the poem:

> Known had I what I knew not
> When we met eye to eye,
> That thenceforth I should view not
> Again beneath the sky
> So truefooted a farer
> As you who faced me then,
> My path had been a rarer
> Than it figures among men! (*P* 806)

This is not one of Hardy's most successful stanzas, but its ending illustrates a device which he often uses to good effect. Hypothesis and uncertainty are frequent in his work, emphasising the fragile hopes of life, the possibilities of sudden calamity and misdirection. Observers and eavesdroppers often appear in the novels: Ladywell observes Picotee from the Weir House (*HE* 21); de Stancy spies on Paula in her gymnasium (*AL* 197); Susan and her daughter watch Henchard presiding over the table at dinner when they come to Casterbridge (*MC* 50); and there are many others. Hardy likes to combine hypothesis and silent observation by presenting a scene as if through the eyes of a nameless spectator, with the syntax of possibility:

> Had a looker-on been posted in the immediate vicinity of the barrow, he would have learned that these persons were boys and men of the neighbouring hamlets. (*RN* 39)

> 'O, an amazing treat!' said Miss Johnson, with an ecstacy in which a close observer might have discovered a tinge of ghastliness. (*TM* 124)

The observer may indeed take on a more active role and behave like a character actively interested in the plot:

> Had a person followed Louis when he withdrew, that watcher would have discovered, on peeping through the key-hole of his door, that he was engaged in one of the oddest occupations for such a man. (*TT* 148)

Hypothesis is often divorced altogether from the personal, and suggests the tentative and 'tremulous' quality of human life which no human agency can control:

> Had this been a case in the court of an omniscient judge he might have entered on his notes the curious fact that Sue had placed the minor for the major indiscretion, and had not said a word about the kiss. (*JO* 184)

The failure or inability of a character to discern the truth is another source of unfulfilled possibility:

> Had he regarded his inner self spectacularly . . . he might have felt pride in the discernment of a somewhat rare power in him – that of keeping not only judgment but emotion suspended in difficult cases. (*W* 49)

> Could he have seen how she made use of those silent hours he might have found reason to reverse his judgment on her quality. (*MC* 128)

The sense of the uncertainty of life and the ultimate control of an uncaring destiny is sometimes heightened by use of the passive voice. The lack of a formal subject draws the reader toward the actual condition which is being suffered. Passive and hypothesis are combined to eerie purpose:

> Could the real have been beheld instead of the corporeal merely, the corner of the room in which he sat would have been filled with a form typical of anxious suspense, large-eyed, tight-lipped, awaiting the issue. (*W* 155)

More often, the passive indicates a bleak actuality:

> Now this hope had been whirled away like thistledown. (*HE* 97)

> That he had been recognized by this man was highly probable; yet there was room for a doubt. (*FFM* 298)

When the letters were posted Jude mentally began to criticize
them; he wished they had not been sent.   (*JO* 93)

Constructions like these put the reader for a moment into the
position of an observer with an overview of the situation; it is a
great strength in Hardy's fiction that he can manipulate our vision
between objective knowledge of the action and a feeling of direct
involvement with the characters until our perceptions merge with
theirs. Immediacy and a sense of being at the author's side as the
story unfolds are sometimes given by use of the present tense.
Hardy uses this sparingly in actual narrative and never attempts
the extended use of the simple present in which Dickens wrote
the third-person sections of *Bleak House*. His brief statements in
the present are usually striking and focus attention on a critical
point of development:

Thus Tess walks on; a figure which is part of the landscape.

(*TD* 269)

It is the popular day, the shilling day, and of the fast arriving
excursion trains two from different directions enter the two
contiguous railway stations at almost the same minute.

(*JO* 245)

Hardy more often uses the present tense to make some authorial
observation of a general truth, exemplified in an incident of the
plot. This is a favourite device of his and one which drew critical
comment in his own time:

Like George Eliot, the author delights in running off to
sententiae, in generalising abstractions out of the special point
in hand. He inclines to this intellectual pastime a little too often,
and with too much of laboured epigram.[2]

Whether the habit is wearisome or makes a significant connection
between the fiction and our experience of reality, is a judgement
which the individual reader must make. It is certainly frequent in
the novels and stories:

Children begin with detail, and learn up to the general;

they begin with the contiguous, and gradually comprehend the universal. *(JO* 235, on 'Father Time')

Observations about the characteristics of women are often made:

> A new-made wife can usually manage to excite interest for a few weeks, even though the prospects of the household ways and means are cloudy. *(JO* 45)

> It may be observed that when a young woman returns a rude answer to a young man's civil remark her heart is in a state which argues rather hopefully for his case than otherwise.
> *(UG* 132)

Sometimes the general observation is about the natural world. As Clym listens to the storm which will destroy Wildeve and Eustacia, Hardy moved from detailed description in the past tense to the comment:

> It was one of those nights when cracks in the walls of old churches widen, when ancient stains on the ceilings of decayed manor-houses are renewed and enlarged from the size of a man's hand to an area of many feet. *(RN* 324)

These interpolations are usually neat and unobtrusive. Occasionally Hardy crashes into the action with both feet, clumsily drawing attention to the artifice of fiction:

> We gain a good view of our heroine as she advances to her place in the ladies' line. *(UG* 71)

> We glance for a moment at the state of affairs on the land they were nearing. *(HE* 269)

> It has been stated that Shaston was the anchorage of a curious and interesting group of itinerants. *(JO* 209)

> The King, as aforesaid, was at the neighbouring town. ('The Melancholy Hussar of the German Leigion')

> He . . . . came indoors, as we have seen, to the fearful shock
> that awaited him.   (*FFM* 270)

Direct address to the reader is, of course, a feature of the Victorian novel which has largely disappeared in the present century as the author withdraws more discreetly from his creation. The rhetorical question was a favourite way of creating rapport, and is one which Hardy uses:

> What was Anne doing?   (*TM* 108)

> Why did a woman of this sort live on Egdon Heath?   (*RN* 83)

> Was Bathsheba altogether blind to the obvious fact that the
> support of a lover's arms is not of the kind best calculated to
> assist a resolve to renounce him?   (*FFM* 195)

Sometimes he speaks directly to the reader, though in general he is more sparing of the device than his predecessors in the novel. 'Reader, I married him' declares Jane Eyre and Dickens begins the last paragraph of *Hard Times* with the apostrophe, 'Dear reader!' In the direct approach as in many other ways Hardy's writing is uneven. He can be formal and heavy even when rising towards perhaps the most tragic and memorable ending in his fiction:

> The last pages to which the chronicler of these lives would ask
> the reader's attention are concerned with the scene in and out
> of Jude's bedroom when leafy summer came round again.
> (*JO* 342)

Yet he can invoke authorial presence with a delicacy which does not intrude on the reality of the character and action but gives an enhanced sense of reality in which author, reader and character are united. One of the finest moments in Hardy's novels comes when Tess has baptised her child and concludes the Prayer Book service:

> Boldly and triumphantly in the stopt-diapason note which her
> voice acquired when her heart was in her speech and which will
> never be forgotten by those who knew her.   (*TD* 109)

The simple past of repeated experience and the future of continuing recall are perfectly combined. Such felicities outweigh the clumsy and tortuous passages in Hardy's writing. A final example will show Hardy at his best, combining several of the features previously discussed:

> As the resting man looked at the barrow, he became aware that its summit, hitherto the highest object in the whole prospect round, was surmounted by something higher. It rose from the semi-globular mound like a spike from a helmet. The first instinct of an imaginative stranger might have been to suppose it the person of one of the Celts who built the barrow, so far had all of modern date withdrawn from the scene. It seemed a sort of last man among them, musing for a moment before dropping into eternal night with the rest of his race. (*RN* 38)

The sentences are kept well under control and balanced in length. The observation of a character moves to that of an imaginary presence, in the syntax of hypothesis. The image of a 'last man' has a phantom, insubstantial presence, existing linguistically as the predicate of the copula *seemed* and governing only participles which lead to falling cadence of the final phrase, alliteration emphasising the strong, monosyllabic close.

8 Dialect

Hardy took a very positive attitude towards the dialect of his native county. For him it was neither a debased form of standard English nor an embellishment to give 'local colour' to his writing, but an ancient tongue with characteristics which existed in their own right and not as deviations. His master here was William Barnes in whose obituary notice he wrote:

> In the systematic study of his native dialect . . . . he has shown the world that far from being, as popularly supposed, a corruption of correct English, it is a distinct branch of Teutonic speech, regular in declension and conjugation, and richer in many classes of words than any other tongue known to him
>
> (*PW* 101)

For himself, he objected to a reviewer of his poems 'saying that because I used a dozen old English words which every true friend of the language is anxious to restore, they were written in a *patois*' (*CL* II 214). He was forced to concede that dialect was declining as the process of national education was 'reducing the speech of this country to uniformity, and obliterating every year many a fine old local word' (*PW* 76).

There was much contemporary criticism of his use of dialect. He was accused of writing dialogue which was difficult to interpret, but also of making his rustic characters speak in too elevated a manner. Coventry Patmore was one of many who found both faults:

> He vacillates between giving an exact facsimile of the village talk and doing what many French novelists think it proper to do – that is to say, putting town talk into the lips of the peasants.[1]

One criticism to which he replied directly was the *Athenaeum* review of *The Return of the Native* which objected that his 'people talk as no people ever talk now'. Hardy made his defence in a subsequent issue:

> An author may be said to fairly convey the spirit of intelligent peasant talk if he retains the idiom, compass and characteristic expressions, although he may not encumber the page with obsolete pronunciations of the purely English words, and with mispronunciations of those derived from Latin and Greek. In the printing of standard speech hardly any phonetic principle at all is observed; and if a writer attempts to exhibit on paper the precise accents of a rustic speaker he disturbs the proper balance of a true representation by unduly insisting upon the grotesque element, thus directing attention to a point of inferior interest, and diverting it from the speaker's meaning.[2]

This was Hardy's attitude in 1878. He was not always closely faithful to it but he had grasped the essential points at issue. He had to contend with the response of readers who associated dialect only with the 'grotesque element' of comic or exaggeratedly 'low' characters. Dickens, dead only a few years, had used cockney speech in this way; Elizabeth Gaskell and George Eliot had given dialect greater dignity, but the old tradition going back to the eighteenth-century novel was still strong. The other danger was the attempt to transcribe local speech so accurately that communication would be lost as the reader struggled with deviant spelling. This had been the problem with Emily Brontë, to a lesser extent with some of Gaskell's dialogue, and notably with Barnes.

Hardy, wisely, did not attempt to create a phonetic system out of the regular alphabet aided by a few diacritical marks. His purpose was not to reproduce in the reader's imagining ear the precise aural experience of listening to Dorset peasants, but to give the impression of how the speech of certain characters differed from the educated norm. In so doing, he did not want to arouse laughter – though there is plenty of humour in some of the rustic scenes – but to suggest levels of status in the community, relationships and emotional responses. He understood that there is 'hardly any phonetic principle at all' in the way that even standard speech is written down, and that the additional sounds of dialect raise extra problems. He knew better than to engage in phonological analysis in the text and was content to write of Tess that she used a dialect of which the 'characteristic intonation' was 'the voicing approximately rendered by the syllable UR, probably as rich an utterance as any to be found in human speech' (*TD* 36). Writing to the French translator of the novel he tried, not very successfully, to be more explicit and suggested '*rh*um much prolonged and deeper . . . . in English the nearest approach I can think of is "uhr". (It is very noticeable in the word "her", which the rustics pronounce "hurrr")' (*CL* VI 76).

Although he had a precise ear and a loving regard for the niceties of Dorset speech, in his novels and poems he used a more impressionistic system, not always consistent, but very effective for his purpose. The dialect which he called 'Wessex' was, like the region, essentially Dorset with traits from other surrounding counties and sometimes even from further afield. It is impossible here to attempt a detailed study of all his methods of reproducing dialogue. A selection will show that he makes his rustic characters deviate from standard expectations in pronunciation, lexis and grammar, and that these deviations are controlled to give emphasis in particular situations.[3]

In pronunciation, Hardy attends to the sounds of dialect speech rather than the stresses and intonation which are more difficult to convey without distracting explanations. A negative, but important, feature is the loss of consonantal sounds, in a cluster of two or more consonants. This often occurs medially to give *ath'art* for 'athwart', *miss'ess* for 'mistress', *pu'pit* for 'pulpit'. It can also be final as *aroun'* for 'around', *wi'* for 'with'; and less often final as initial as *'ithout* for 'without'. Sometimes Hardy removes a medial consonant where it would not normally be pronounced in southern speech, perhaps to emphasise the shortness of the vowels as *nothen* for 'northern' and, a frequent form, *p'ason* for 'parson'.

The voicing of certain consonants, giving *v* for *f* and *z* for *s* is a traditional feature of south-western English. Shakespeare uses it in *King Lear* when Edgar, pretending to be a peasant, says to Oswald 'let poor volk pass' (IV v 236). Hardy writes forms like *vlee, vrom, voot*, and *zilver, zummer, Zunday*.

Vowel sounds show some regular characteristics of change: a common one is the movement of [i] to [e] giving 'spirit' as *sperrit*. The long vowel [i:] becomes a diphthong, close to [ei] but a little more open, as *craters* for 'creatures'; Gabriel Oak refuses the offer of a 'clane cup' and is assured that the grit on a piece of bacon which has been dropped is 'clane dirt' (*FFM* 69). The back vowel [ɔ:] is opened to [a] so that the King is hailed as 'King Jarge' (*TM* 97) and ordinary folk are 'poor martels' (*UG* 89). An extra vowel is sometimes inserted in the spelling to show that a long vowel is being given longer duration, as 'tunes' becomes *tuens* and 'cakes' *keakes*, and almost separating into two syllables. Barnes had used the diaresis for this effect, writing *meäke, gäy*. A variant which seems to have endured in Dorset was standard at an earlier time. Hardy makes an old soldier tell how:

> They bore my wownded frame to camp,
> And shut my gapèn skull, and washed en cleän,
> And jined en wi' a zilver clamp
> Thik night at Valencieën. (*P* 20)

This short stanza contains several of the dialect pointers which have already been mentioned, with examples of Hardy's rare use of the diaresis favoured by Barnes. The spelling *wownded* shows 'wounded' pronounced as if to rhyme with 'sounded' and this was once the normal pronunciation: in the middle of the seventeenth century Montrose rhymes *sounds* and *wounds*. The spelling *jined* for 'joined' equates with Pope's rhyme of *join* and *divine* in the early eighteenth century.

Other deviant spellings are more conventional indications of colloquial speech, such as weakened forms like *'tis, 'twere*. Spellings like *nater* for 'nature' and *winder* for 'window' suggest careless rather than distinctively local pronunciations; Dickens uses both of these forms for speakers from different parts of England. Others again are closer to standard colloquial speech than the careful emphasis suggested by regular spelling. Syncopic forms like *b'lieve, o'* and *penneth* ('pennyworth') are of this type, and *carrel* gives the weak final vowel of 'carol' better than orthography. The convention is still used by novelists who write *sez* and *wot* to show uneducated speech, though these are actually closer to what most people, at least in the southern part of Britain, say in relaxed speech.[4] It is possible that standard pronunciation was more precise than it is today and that these weakenings would have been more deviant; certainty eludes us in many questions of pronunciation before the era of reliable recording and phonetic analysis. For instance, Phillotson calls Sue *Soo* and Hardy comments, 'this being the way in which he pronounced her name' (*JO* 184). Whether this is a residual dialect pronunciation or Phillotson's idiophonic rendering is disputed; all that we can be sure of is that Hardy himself regarded [sju:] as normal.

The dialect effect, of course, comes not from isolated words but from a combination of deviant spellings. Two examples will show how Hardy presents rustic speech in such a way as to make it distinctive but not inaccessible to interpretation. First, William Worm, Swancourt's servant:

> Would ye mind coming round by the back way? The front door is got stuck wi' the wet, as he will do sometimes; and the Turk can't open en. I know I am only a poor wambling man that 'ill never pay the Lord for my making, sir; but I can show the way in, sir. (*PBE* 46)

Second, from 'The Bride-Night Fire', one of the few poems which Hardy wrote wholly in dialect:

> 'I think I mid almost ha' borne it,' she said,
> 'Had my griefs one by one come to hand;
> But O, to be slave to thik husbird for bread,
> And then, upon top o' that, driven to wed,
> And then, upon top o' that, burnt out o' bed,
> Is more than my nater can stand!'

It is clear that the reader unfamiliar with Dorset speech will receive an impression rather than a close transcription; also that Hardy conveys dialect through lexis and syntax as well as pronunciation. He valued the words of his native county and defended their use in poetry. He wrote in the preface to *Wessex Poems* in 1898:

> Whenever an ancient and legitimate word of the district, for which there was no equivalent in received English, suggested itself as the most natural, nearest, and often only expression of a thought, it has been made use of, on what seemed good grounds.

In fiction and specifically dialect poems Hardy used local words even when there was an 'equivalent in received English'. Some are particular favourites, often recurring and made effective by an automatic assurance that we are in the region of Wessex. Among them are *bide*, 'remain' and *homealong*, 'homewards'. The first of these causes little difficulty to readers even today as an archaic form which exists in the passive but not the active vocabulary. Less familiar, but certainly 'ancient and legitimate' are words derived from Old English like *barton*, 'farmyard'; *coomb*, 'valley'; *dorp*, 'village'. Others are mispronunciations of standard words imperfectly grasped by the speaker; such are *mischty*, 'mischief', *maphrotight*, 'hermaphrodite' and the stoutly British rather than notably Dorset rendering of the French *Hôtel Beau-Sèjour* as 'the Hotel Bold Soldier' (*HE* 215).

Other words are less accessible and require a glossary or the notes which are provided in some modern editions. Such are *durn, larry, rafted, shrammed, sumple, vamp, wanzing*. Sometimes an explanation appears in the text, as when a country girl cannot buy *chippols* in London until it is explained that 'they call them young onions here' (*HE* 122). Some words become clear enough in context: it is not hard to read stupidity into 'The little stunpoll of a fellow couldn't call to mind' (*DR* 184) or the general sense of messiness when tapping a barrel of cider becomes 'a squizzling and squirting job' (*UG* 40). Words of very local currency may need authorial comment, like the Portland words *kimberlin* and *lerret* in *The Well-Beloved*.

Idioms may give pause to the reader, even if the individual words are familiar. The phrase *good-now* was explained by Hardy as an intensive, 'like the American "I guess" or "you may be sure",' (*CL* I 277); it is used in *Hamlet* (I i 69) though not quite with this force:

Good now, sit down, and tell me, he that knows.

Other local phrases are 'call home' for the publication of banns of marriage; 'go snacks with' for sharing; 'mops and brooms' for the disorder of senses after heavy drinking.

In grammar also the deviations may in fact be survivals of older usage. When Grammer Oliver refuses to see the doctor with 'Ch woll not have him' (*W* 120), she is speaking something close to Old English. Hardy claimed that forms like 'Ick woll' and 'er war' were still being used by old people in 1888 but were 'dying rapidly' (*CL* I 181), but he incurred some unpopularity as late as 1915 by remarking on the kinship of such forms with modern German in the poem 'The Pity Of It'. Sometimes it is difficult to be certain if the spelling represents deviance in a grammatical form or in pronunciation, as when *'a* stands for 'he' or 'I' and *en* for 'him'. There is firmer ground with the second person singular, used familiarly to one person as it had been universally in English at an earlier time, with pronouns *thy, thou* and verbal forms *wast, dostn't, how'st do*? Inconsistency of usage between singular and plural forms probably reflects the true situation of change: Fancy Day warns her father to avoid the *thou* forms as 'so very humiliating to persons of newer taste' (*UG* 204).

Other verbal usages include *be* as a personed verb ('I be', 'we be') and weak past forms of strong verbs like *knowed, feeled, seed* or *zeed*. Confusions of number may be part of general uneducated usage rather than specific to Dorset: 'mis'ess have sent', 'his grandfer were just such a nice unparticular man' (*FFM* 69). The same may be said of the present tense for past events: 'says she'. Disregard of case in pronouns – 'hard for she', 'nothing to I' is more distinctive of the traditional south-western speech. The double negative comes from the Middle English use of more than one negative to intensify not to destroy the denial and still survives in cockney. Geoffrey Day relates how bees 'got into my shirt and wouldn't be quiet nohow' (*UG* 165).

The real interest of Hardy's use of dialect lies not in his specific indicators, of which these are only a few, but rather in his allocation of dialect features to characters according to their position and contextual situation. A casual listener in the Dorset of his novels would probably not have distinguished clearly between speakers, except when broad dialect caused difficulty in understanding. The majority of the characters may be assumed to have the local accent in some degree. Within the rural community there was, in fact, considerable awareness of status which could make people concerned about their own way of speaking. The prestige of a national standard was growing in the second half of the nineteenth century. The implications for the status-conscious in a dialect area were interesting and often amusing.

Hardy sometimes shows those implications quite overtly. It is usually deviation in grammar or lexis rather than pronunciation that is noticed, and this bears out the supposition that the sound of speech was less often noticed by those brought up to hear it daily. A son with a public school education impatiently corrects his mother who says that the Father 'have been so comfortable . . . that I am sure he cannot have missed us' ('The Son's Veto'). Mrs Dewy, who is thought to have some characteristics of Hardy's mother, objects to her husband calling potatoes *taties* 'in such a work-folk way . . . with our family 'twas never less than "taters", and very often "pertatoes" outright' (*UG* 80). The most notable example is Henchard's fury at Elizabeth-Jane's saying 'bide where you be':

'Bide where you be,' he echoed sharply. 'Good God, are you only fit to carry wash to a pig-trough, that ye use such words as those?'

She reddened with shame and sadness.

'I meant, "Stay where you are," father,' she said in a low, humble voice, 'I ought to have been more careful'

(*MC* 125).

The scene is a shrewd linguistic comment on Henchard's aspirations to status and his personal insecurity; he lapses into the dialect *ye* in his indignation. A mixture of humour and pathos appears in the poem 'The Ruined Maid' when the girl from the country meets an old friend who has become a London prostitute and is awed by her speech:

'At home in the barton you said "thee" and "thou",
And "thik oon" and "theäs oon", and "t'other"; but now
Your talking quite fits 'ee for high compan-ny!' –
'Some polish is gained with one's ruin', said she.

The comparative status of characters may be suggested without comment. Servants speak more broadly than their employers, even if the latter are themselves of humble rank. Giles Winterbourne shows few dialect pointers, but his man Creedle can say 'Lord, lord! if they bain't come a'ready' (*W* 80). The old shepherd with whom Jude and Sue seek shelter when they are too late to return to Melchester speaks in contrast to their standard diction:

'You can bide here, you know, over the night – can't 'em, mother? The place is welcome to ye. 'Tis hard lying, rather, but volk may do worse.' (*JO* 115)

The town constables of Casterbridge use dialect words – 'what can we two poor lammigers do against such a multitude' – while the magistrates who are themselves local tradesmen show little or no trace of dialect. Henchard, who achieves almost standard speech in his time of success, reverts to dialect as his fortunes fall and he becomes an employed man again:

'A fellow of his age going to be Mayor, indeed! . . . But 'tis her money that floats en upward. Ha-ha – how cust odd it is. Here be I, his former master, working for him as man, and he the man standing as master.' (*MC* 203)

We should not assume naturalism in such forms of speech; personal speech-habits do not change so rapidly. Hardy's effect is pragmatic, showing changes of status and relationship by linguistic means, centred on the dialect which he knew so well. The matter is complicated by the presence of certain literary conventions. Although Hardy eschewed the custom of giving broad dialect only to comic or low characters, he sometimes uses it for the 'rustic chorus' which comments on the action, or for minor characters who have a brief and incidental appearance in contrast to the stable role of the principals. A passing cottager, seeing Jude's bonfire of his books, comments, 'Burning up your awld aunt's rubbidge, I suppose?' (*JO* 182); one of the men who accompany Melbury to search for Grace demands 'a mossel and a drop of summat to strengthen our nerves afore we vamp all the way back again' (*W* 320). The stay-lace vendor who witnesses Henchard's sale of his wife comments in broad dialect:

'I glory in the women's sperrit. I'd ha' done it myself – od send if I wouldn't, if a husband had behaved so to me! I'd go, and 'a might call till his keacorn was raw; but I'd never come back'. (*MC* 36)

Conversely, there is the convention of the earlier Victorian novel that virtuous characters or those who are meant fully to engage the reader's sympathy should speak standard English. Dickens had so treated Oliver Twist, Pip and Lizzie Hexam, among others, and Hardy gives little or no dialect to characters like Jude, Giles Winterbourne, and Diggory Venn. Despite an occasional *'ee* or *'em*, the child Jude speaks as unrealistically as Oliver: 'Where is this beautiful city, aunt – this place where Mr. Phillotson is gone to? (*JO* 10). In dealing with Tess, Hardy attempts an explanation which may not be entirely convincing but which he puts to good use in the novel and which suggests his practice with other leading characters:

> Mrs. Durbeyfield habitually spoke the dialect; her daughter, who had passed the Sixth Standard in the National School under a London-trained mistress, spoke two languages; the dialect at home, more or less; ordinary English abroad and to persons of quality. (*TD* 41)

In the earlier, serial version of the book, the passage is different and continues after 'London-trained mistress' to say that Tess spoke dialect 'only when excited by joy, surprise, or grief'. Reversion to dialect under the pressure of emotion is more realistic, and conforms with Hardy's method. When Tess returns home after leaving Angel Clare she shows more dialect signs – 'I don't know how to tell 'ee, mother . . . that's where my misery do lie!' (*TD* 249). Gabriel Oak, who normally shows the fairly standard speech of a leading and sympathetic character changes in passionate talk with Bathsheba:

> If wild heat had to do wi' it, making ye long to overcome the awkwardness about your husband's vanishing, it mid be wrong; but a cold-hearted agreement to oblige a man seems different, somehow. The real sin, ma'am, in my mind, lies in thinking of ever wedding wi' a man you don't love honest and true'. (*FFM* 306)

On the other hand, characters conversing calmly and intimately often show little trace of dialect, even those who might realistically be assumed to have it. When Henchard speaks normally with his returned wife and supposed daughter, none of them uses dialect beyond occasional forms like *ye*. Tess and the other milkmaids at

Talbothays speak similarly; in these and many other such situations the reader needs no distraction from the subject of conversation and does not 'hear' any deviant speech, just as the speakers in their situation would not notice what would be striking to an outsider. We are brought into the scene as silent participants and no more is needed.

A character may lose dialect when he or she takes on a specific role in the action which stretches beyond personality. The furmity woman who is the agent of Henchard's first downfall speaks dialect in her early appearance; when she is in court at Casterbridge she becomes an agent of doom and accusation and her speech becomes almost normal. The constable alleges that she had said to him, 'Dost hear, old turmit-head?', but she gives her evidence in a different tone – 'A man and a woman and with a little child came into my tent . . . they sat down and had a basin apiece' (*MC* 182). This is dramatically right; it is the tension of the court and the coming revelation which engages the reader and not any idiosyncrasies of the participants. At other times the sudden intrusion of dialect may itself heighten tension. The quarrel of Jude and Arabella over the pig-killing is depicted with no trace of dialect on his part, and little on hers; then the outside world breaks in with the broad tone of the professional slaughterer in unconscious irony, 'Well done, young married volk! I couldn't have carried it out much better myself, cuss me if I could!' (*JO* 51).

Hardy then uses dialect not simply for a realistic representation of rustic speech but in many ways which contribute to the effect of his fiction. Some times indeed the purpose may be purely comic, as when the local clergyman is attempting to improve the diction of the choir who sing:

'The Lard looked down vrom Heav'n's high tower!'
'Ah, that's where we are so defective – the pronunciation', interrupted the parson. 'Now repeat after me: "The Lord look'd down from Heav'ns high tower".' The choir repeated like an exaggerated echo: 'The Lawd look'd daown from Heav'n's high towah!' (*TT* 15)

The effect may also be to heighten tragedy, as simple grief is made articulate in natural tones. Thus Creedle, normally comic in his dialect, becomes deeply moving as he mourns for Giles:

'Now I've seen the end of the family, which we can ill afford to lose, wi' such a scanty lot of good folk in Hintock as we've got. And now Robert Creedle will be nailed up in parish boards 'a b'lieve; and nobody will glutch down a sigh for he!' (*W* 288)

Hardy makes little attempt at representing any dialect except that of 'Wessex'. Despite his frequent residence in London, he does not give cockney speech to characters in the London scenes of his novels, although he offered a comic rendering of a cockney bus conductor's comment on women cyclists, in a letter to his sister;

'Oh nao: their sex perfects them. We dares not drive over them wotever they do, and they do jist wot they likes'
(*CL* II 193)

He suggests an Irish porter with 'She's been very queer, saur . . . sending messages down the spakin'-tube' (*WB* 85), but generally leaves the work to the reader; 'he spoke in a strange northern accent' (*TD* 309) or, 'the accent was not quite that of an Englishman, and struck him as hailing from one of the Channel Islands' (*WB* 137). The only extended attempt outside Wessex is the accent of Farfrae in *The Mayor of Casterbridge*, represented conventionally, but quite effectively:

'It is true I am in the corren trade – but I have replied to no advairrtisment, and arranged to see no one. I am on my way to Bristol – from there to the other side of the warrld'.
(*MC* 61)

Farfrae's speech shows the same dramatic traits as those of other characters in the book, decreasing in relaxed intimacy and becoming stronger under the pressure of emotion. At ease with Henchard his rolled *r* disappears: 'I'll be glad to hear it, if I can be of any service', but returns in anger at Henchard's treatment of Abel Whittle: 'For maircy's sake, what object's this?' and in sympathy for Henchard's misfortune: 'It's the way of the warrld' (*MC* 85, 102, 201). In a later preface to the novel, Hardy defended the representation of Farfrae's speech in a statement which illuminates his use of south-western dialect as well:

> It must be remembered that the Scotchman of the tale is represented not as he would appear to other Scotchmen, but as he would appear to people of outer regions. Moreover, no attempt is made herein to reproduce his entire pronunciation phonetically, any more than that of the Wessex speakers.

Hardy's position on dialect in fiction was the same in 1912 as it had been in his reply to the *Athenaeum* review in 1878.

He loved the Dorset speech best and could hear it even in the sounds of nature, as he suggests in the charming and mischievous poem, 'The Spring Call':

> Down Wessex way, when spring's a-shine,
>   The blackbird's 'pret-ty de-urr!'
> In Wessex accents marked as mine
>   Is heard afar and near.
>
> He flutes it strong, as if in song
>   No R's of feebler tone
> Than his appear in 'pretty dear',
>   Have blackbirds ever known.

He wonders if Scottish Blackbirds sing 'prattie deerh', London ones 'pehty de-aw' and Irish 'purrity dare'; but:

> Yes, in this clime at pairing time.
>   As soon as eyes can see her
> At dawn of day, the proper way
>   To call is 'pret-ty de-urr!'

9 Forms of Speech

Conversation is an important element in fiction, as it is in life. One of the tests of quality in a novelist is the skill with which dialogue between characters is presented. In reading dialogue, we feel particularly close to the 'reality' with which the novel is linked: it is a fragile link, easily broken by anything that strikes us as artificial. Some writers, of course, make no pretence at illusion, but continually draw attention to the fact that what they are writing is fiction; this is not Hardy's way, and the reader is expected to enter into the story without disbelief during the time of reading. When characters are supposed to be talking, the reader is in the position of a silent listener, following the conversation rather like one of the eavesdroppers whom Hardy is fond of introducing into the plot.

Even in the novel of extreme realism, dialogue is not simply a reproduction in writing of what would be heard by a listener. An unseen tape-recorder reveals that speech never has the smoothness and order which we expect in a novel. Everyday speech is full of repetitions, hesitations, changes of construction and unfinished sentences; indeed, not all speech utterances conform to the grammarian's idea of a sentence at all. We support our words with extra noises of satisfaction, doubt or annoyance, and supplement their meaning with facial expressions and sometimes bodily gestures. Conversation is in fact a more dynamic, and less purely verbal, activity than can well appear on a printed page. The novelist has to take account of these non-verbal elements and try to convey them verbally. Without any additional pointers, the words of dialogue become dull; with too many, the sense and continuity is lost. Anthony Trollope summed up the novelist's problem:

The novel-writer in constructing his dialogue must so steer between absolute accuracy of language – which would give to his conversation an air of pedantry, and the slovenly inaccuracy of ordinary talkers, which if closely followed would offend by an appearance of grimace – as to produce upon the ear of his readers a sense of reality. If he be quite real he will seem to attempt to be funny. If he be quite correct he will seem to be unreal.[1]

We must remember that it is hard to know what was natural speech in earlier periods. Until the recent advent of recording and an accurate notation for transcribing speech, there is little evidence for how people spoke except that of literature. Flashes of conversation set down in letters or memoirs are our only supplement to what writers have imaginatively done with the speaking voice. Fictional dialogue is influenced not only by the general process of tidying the eliminating features that would be intolerable in reading, but also by the constraints of contemporary fashions and conventions. Until recently, most swearwords could not be printed, and we have seen that virtuous characters in fiction are often given educated speech irrespective of their social position.

Careful use of the available written evidence, supplemented by the fuller records of the twentieth century, suggest that conversation has tended to become less formal and more casual in expression. It is probable that much of the polite speech of the nineteenth century would sound stilted to modern ears and that even informal conversation was less laconic and familiar than our modern expectation. Nevertheless, it has to be said that Hardy is not always convincing in his dialogue; the tendency to elaborate syntax and recondite words which he shows in narrative sometimes overtakes his characters. He had a high view of fictional speech and was critical of novelists who 'use the phrases of the season, present or past, with absolute accuracy as to idiom, expletive, slang . . . In aiming at the trivial and the ephemeral they have almost surely missed better things' (*PW* 119). His sense of the dignity of speech appropriate for serious themes can produce magnificent dialogue; it can also lead him into banality. Edmund Gosse wrote in exasperation, 'Sue and Jude talk a sort of University Extension jargon that breaks the heart'.[2]

Hardy was aware that avoidance of the ephemeral could lead to the unnatural. He wrote to an amateur author, Lady Grove:

> I fancy your madman rather too melodramatic. Such phrases as 'Avaunt, fiend!' 'Speak, woman', etc., would not be used by any modern human being, even were he as mad as ten hatters. (*CL* II 189).

To begin with the debit side before looking at Hardy's special virtues, we can see him falling into artificiality when he wants to be serious. With all allowances for change in conversational style, it is hard to believe that one man could speak to his brother about their sister like this:

> She promises to be a most attractive, not to say beautiful, girl. I have seen that for years; and if her face is not her fortune, her face and brain together will be, if I observe and contrive aright. That she should be every inch of her, an accomplished and refined woman, was indispensible for the fulfilment of her destiny, and for moving onwards and upwards with us. ('A Tragedy of Two Ambitions')

Were even Victorian proposals couched in the terms with which Maybold addresses Fancy Day:

> O Fancy, I have watched you, criticized you even severely, brought my feelings to the light of judgment, and still have found them rational, and such as any man might have expected to be inspired with by a woman like you! So there is nothing hurried, secret, or untoward in my desire to do this. Fancy, will you marry me? (*UG* 183)

Extreme feeling might cause extremity of language, but a leisurely ride in the woods seems unlikely to produce extracts from a manual on the aesthetics of nature:

> Abner Power was quite sentimental that day. 'In such places as these', he said, as he rode alongside Mrs. Goodman, 'nature's

powers in the multiplication of one type strike me as much as the grandeur of the mass.'

Mrs. Goodman agreed with him, and Paula said, 'The foliage forms the roof of an interminable green crypt, the pillars being the trunks, and the vault the inter-lacing boughs'.   (*AL* 319)

One understands Gosse's criticism when Sue speaks to Jude thus:

'Well,' she sighed, 'you've owned that it would probably end in misery for us. And I am not so exceptional a woman as you think. Fewer women like marriage than you suppose, only they enter into it for the dignity it is assumed to confer, and the social advantages it gains them – a dignity and an advantage that I am quite willing to do without'.   (*JO* 221)

Passages like these can be found in all the novels, but they are not Hardy's norm. Most of his dialogue expresses the characters within their situation and draws the reader with it. Often there is a sense of ease and naturalness which overcomes the barrier of time. When Fanny Robin speaks to Troy through his barrack window, the brief, simple exchanges well convey the pathos of the scene:

'How did you come here?'
'I asked which was your window. Forgive me!'
'I did not expect you to-night. Indeed, I did not think you would come at all. It was a wonder you found me here. I am orderly tomorrow.'
'You said I was to come.'
'Well – I said that you might.'
'Yes, I mean that I might. You are glad to see me, Frank?'
'O yes – of course.' (*FFM* 93f)

Here, and often in Hardy's pages, we have the sense of listening to a real conversation. Only a few examples can be given, but no reader of Hardy can miss the strength of his dialogue at its best. When Henchard tells Farfrae about Lucetta, we share the tension and feel with both the men, marked by traces of dialect which do not obtrude:

'Do you remember my story of that second woman – who suffered for her thoughtless intimacy with me?'

'I do,' said Farfrae.

'Do you remember my telling 'ee how it all began and how it ended?'

'Yes.'

'Well, I have offered to marry her now that I can; but she won't marry me. Now what would you think of her – I put it to you?'

'Well, ye owe her nothing now,' said Farfrae heartily.

'It is true,' said Henchard, and went on.   (*MC* 165)

Two sisters discuss the possibility of one of them marrying an elderly peer:

'Such an old man too; I wouldn't have him for the world.'

'Don't jump at conclusions so absurdly, Picotee. Why wouldn't you have him for the world?'

'Because he is old enough to be my grandfather, and yours too.'

'Indeed he is not; he is only middle-aged.'

'O, Berta! Sixty-five at least.'

'He may or may not be that; and if he is, it is not old. He is so entertaining that one forgets all about age in connection with him.' (*HE* 174)

Words alone do not create convincing dialogue. The author must occasionally intervene to comment on the manner of speaking and the reactions of the participants in the conversation. Descriptive language can become tedious and detract from continuity if it is excessive. Hardy manages this with competence; he has no outstanding or experimental methods of approach but is a sound craftsman. The effect can be shown by the simple addition of an adverb:

'Oh, very well,' said the deep voice indifferently.   (*FFM* 84)

'Stupid? O no!' said Farfrae gravely.   (*MC* 157)

'Ah – you are vexed!' she said regretfully.   (*JO* 144)

'May nobody wish him more harm in that exercise than I do!' said Somerset fervently.   (*AL* 292)

Longer descriptive phrases may be used, with the danger of making authorial intervention too obvious:

'You make me very uneasy and sorry by writing such things!' she murmured, suddenly dropping the mere *caqueterie* of a fashionable first introduction, and speaking with some of the dudgeon of a child towards a severe schoolmaster.   (*PBE* 185)

'You should try,' replied the widow from the serene heights of a soul conscious not only of spiritual but of social superiority.
(*JO* 265)

The words and manner of speech are aided by *prosodic* features: stress, intonation, pitch and so on. These can be shown by variations in spelling or devices of typography like italicising or capital letters. Writers have developed a number of conventions through which the written code can accommodate aural effects. Here, too, Hardy is skilful but not innovative. Extra spacing can show the effect of a name prolonged by calling: 'Gra-a-ce!' (*W* 150), or of children crying: 'Tess won't go-o-o and be made a la-a-dy of! – no, she says she wo-o-on't!' (*TD* 64), or of a shouted word of command: 'Mar-r-r-rch!' (*TM* 165). Emphasis can be shown visually and conveyed by comment:

'Certainly not!' he replied. He pronounced the inhibition lengthily and sonorously, so that the 'not' sounded like 'n-o-o-o-t!'   (*PBE* 114)

This is conventional; Hardy shows more strength in another area of speech, the *phonational*. No two voices sound exactly alike, even speaking the same words with shared emphasis and accent. Hardy is very sensitive to the individual qualities of voices, particularly those of women, and makes us 'hear' them through his descriptions. Phonational qualities may be permanent, part of the personal voice pattern. Christian Cantle has 'a thin jibbering voice'

(*RN* 47); Martin Cannister 'a tenor tongue' (*PBE* 250); Angel is first attracted to Tess by her 'fluty voice' (*TD* 131). The quality of Sue Brideshead's voice is noticed throughout the story in which she appears. It is 'positive and silvery', but 'tremulous' (*JO* 81); later we hear 'a contralto note of tragedy coming suddenly into her silvery voice' (123); when she is unhappy her words are 'lifelessly spoken' (158): and the 'tragic contralto note' comes back 'as of old' (171). An unnamed girl in a poem has a voice which shares Tess's quality:

> And her sweet syllables seemed to play
> Like flute-notes softly blown. (*P* 412)

Less romantically, a speaker may be known by his stammer:

> 'P-p-p-p-pl-pl-pl-pl-l-l-l-ease, ma'am . . . '
> 'A's a stammering man, mem,' said Henery Fray in an under-
> tone. (*FFM* 87)

Distinctive qualities of voice may be temporary; perhaps caused by drunkenness:

> 'I've-got-a-gr't-family-vault-at-Kingsbere – and knighted-fore-
> fathers-in-lead-coffins-there!' (*TD* 35)

> 'As-one-of-Majesty's servants-care-Majesty's mails-duty-put
> letters-own hands.' (*DR* 342)

Speech may be affected by shock: when Chickerel recognises Ethelberta at the dinner party he speaks 'in a husky voice, scarcely above a whisper' (*HE* 262); or by injury, when Fitzpiers speaks 'in a difficult whisper' (*W* 238); or emotion, as when Eustacia speaks 'huskily' after the death of Mrs Yeobright (*RN* 279). The changes can be described more graphically: Giles's voice becomes 'as husky as that of the leaves under foot': Picotee in distress has 'tears in her eyes and quavers in her voice' (*MC* 190). It is to be noted that Hardy, like most other writers, does not attempt complete consistency or accuracy in these matters; the drunken Durbeyfield would be unlikely to articulate 'knighted forefathers' fully, but that is not the point: it is an impression, not a phonetic transcript that is being created.

Communication is not effected only through words and tones. A good deal is done through laughter, sighs and other extra-lingual sounds which form part of the agreed code. Hardy shows a keen understanding of how these work, and some ingenuity in representing them. He is particularly good on the different types of laughter, for which the lexis gives words like 'giggle', 'chuckle', 'guffaw'. In the dialogue quoted above between Picotee and Ethelberta, Picotee continues her objections to Lord Mountclere by saying, 'He laughs like this – "Hee-hee-hee!"' (*HE* 174). There is acute observation of how laughter sounds different from various voices when Tess leaves her companions to go with Alec:

> 'Ho-ho-ho!' laughed dark Car.
> 'Hee-hee-hee!' laughed the tippling bride, as she steadied herself on the arm of her fond husband.
> 'Heu-heu-heu!' laughed dark Car's mother.   (*TD* 84)

The landlord who witnesses Dick Dewy's courting of Fancy laughs:

> 'Heu-heu! hay-hay, Master Dewy? Ho-ho!'   (*UG* 140)

Degrees of laughter are nicely matched with character and response:

> 'Haw, haw, haw!' laughed Martin Cannister, who had heard the explanation of this striking story for the hundredth time.
> 'Huh, huh, huh!' laughed John Smith, who had heard it for the thousandth.
> 'Hee, hee, hee!' laughed William Worm, who had never heard it at all, but was afraid to say so.   (*PBE* 257)

Other extra-lingual sounds feature in Hardy's fiction. He is fond of the representation 'Piph-h-h-h' to show sharp exhalation of breath after the exertion of dancing (*UG* 76), or bellringing (*DR* 415), or to show response to a hot day (*PBE* 169). More traditional in fiction are 'Ssh!' to enjoin silence; 'Faugh!' or 'Ugh!' to show distaste; 'Tcht, tcht' for the rapid click of the tongue that registers annoyance. Slightly more unusual is Hardy's observation of the click in the speech of an old person, perhaps suggesting the impediment of loss of teeth: 'kik' or 'clk' characterises the speech of Grandfather Cantle (*RN* 50), old Derriman (*TM* 171) and Tranter Dewy (*UG* 101). These enliven the passages of dialogue and are sometimes supplemented or replaced by verbal description. Some of Hardy's best moments are in his imaginative responses to human sounds. When Mrs Charmond yawns, 'Marty heard a gentle oral sound, soft as a breeze' (*W* 55); Mr Swancourt lies in bed 'puffing and fizzing like a bursting bottle' (*PBE* 40); Lord Mountclere 'sighed like a poet over a ledger' (*HE* 239).

In all these aspects of dialect Hardy generally follows the normal fictional practice of direct speech. Quotation marks indicate what purport to be the actual words used by the characters, chosen by them in the conversational situation. Speech may also be rendered indirectly, incorporated into the narrative. This has the effect of giving more emphasis to the plot and by implication to the controlling omniscience of the author, than to the characters themselves. Hardy's people usually speak their own words; his use of reported speech is rare and has no particular quality of distinction:

> She would read if he wished, she said; she was in no hurry. (*TM* 58)

> He occasionally came in to see if the fire was burning, to ask her if she wanted anything, to tell her that the wind had shifted from south to west, to ask her if she would like him to gather her some blackberries; to all which inquiries she replied to the negative or with indifference. (*RN* 304)

Another method is the 'free indirect style', which puts speech into the reported form but keeps some of the syntax of direct speech and some of the character's idiolect. This style, popular with Jane Austen and Dickens among others, is not often used by Hardy but is occasionally effective:

> The dairyman, though he had thought of dismissing her soon, now made a great concern about losing her. What should he do about his skimming? Who would make the

ornamental butter-pats for the Anglebury and Sandbourne
ladies?   (*TD* 202)

Thus Crick receives the news of Tess's coming marriage: she
remains the centre of interest and his direct voice is not heard,
but the interrogative forms and suggestion of his own idiom
make his background presence vivid and suggest the ripples
which a personal decision spreads as far as distant towns. When
Lucetta is asked if she knows Farfrae, her caution and reserve
are shown by withholding her direct voice but making it heard
distinctively:

O yes, she knew him, she declared; she could not help knowing
almost everybody in Casterbridge, living in such a gazebo over
the centre and arena of the town.   (*MC* 166)

A similar reserve is shown in Paula's unexpected meeting with
Somerset; the free indirect style distances her and yet makes her
present in the phrases of embarrassed formality:

She declared that this was an unexpected pleasure. Had he
arranged to come on the tenth as she wished? How strange
that they should meet thus! – and yet not strange – the world
was so small.   (*AL* 239)

Indirect speech is also used for conveying characters' thoughts.
Before the twentieth-century experiments of Virginia Woolf and
James Joyce in the stream of consciousness and interior monologue, thoughts in fiction had to be conveyed as speech, either
as if directly overheard or as if formalised by the narrator. Hardy
uses both methods; thus Angel reflects:

She is a dear, dear Tess, he thought to himself, as one
deciding on the true construction of a difficult passage. 'Do
I realize solemnly enough how utterly and irretrievably this
little womanly thing is the creature of my good or bad faith
and fortune?'   (*TD* 215)

Dick Dewy's reflections on love come in a free indirect mode:

Of course the Angel was not to blame – a young woman
living alone in a house could not ask him indoors unless she
had known him better – he should have kept her outside before
floundering into that final farewell. (*UG* 84)

When Jude thinks bitterly about his condition, his thoughts
are reported in a formal, almost stilted manner; it is Hardy's
comment on marriage rather than the character's silent verbalising
that we hear:

Their lives were ruined, he thought; ruined by the funda-
mental error of their matrimonial union: that of having based
a permanent contract on a temporary feeling which had no
necessary connection with affinities that alone render a life-long
comradeship tolerable. (*JO* 54)

In these passages, Hardy shows skill and versatility in managing
the language at his disposal, but little that cannot be found in other
writers of the period. His recording ear and his sensitivity to social
nuances, always apparent in the events of his fiction, are used to
great effect in another way. We all know that communication
through speech does not depend solely on the 'message' which
has to be conveyed. How we frame the message is influenced
by relationship with others in the conversation: the degree of
intimacy, differences of age and status, personal feelings before
the conversation begins. We do not speak in exactly the same
way to our close relatives, our working colleagues, a stranger
encountered by chance or a small child. The variations are those
of *register*: the choice of language according to the social situation
in which it is being used. The pointers of register vary between
different languages; the familiar *tu* is used to one person known
intimately, or perhaps treated as very young or inferior, in French,
while *vous* is used to one person in more formal address as well
as in the plural. We have no such distinction in modern English,
though *thou* once had similar implications. Today we depend more
on choice of words than on grammatical differences, aided by
factors like intonation, and the actual number of words it seems
necessary to use for politeness.

Differences of register, though far from extinct, have declined
as society has become less ranked and social contacts less formal.

In the nineteenth century there was more scope for register, to reflect a much stronger sense of comparative status and relationship. Through the words of his characters, Hardy reveals a great deal about the period, both in the rural community and in London. Something has been said already about the way in which dialect is used to show the position of speakers in the rural hierarchy; this is an area in which Hardy excels. In addition to dialect features, or in speech without them, he conveys a fine sense of the regular social situation and of changing relationships within it.

The use of *sir* to a man considered to be of higher rank, or to a stranger of equal rank, was almost obligatory in Victorian England. Thus Grace Melbury, speaking to a childhood companion, cannot forget the girls at the boarding school which she has attended, 'whose parents Giles would have addressed with a deferential Sir or Madam' (*W* 56). Havill uses it to a fellow-architect 'with a mixed manner of cordiality, contempt, and misgiving' – 'You have a practice, I suppose, sir?' (*AL* 99). Change in a man's status can affect old relationships; John Smith calls his successful son Stephen, arrived from London, 'sir', and comments:

' "Sir", says I to my own son! but ye've gone up so, Stephen.' (*PBE* 251)

Perhaps even stranger to modern ears, women may use this polite address to men, outside a commercial relationship. Elizabeth-Jane, affected by Farfrae's new status in Casterbridge, says 'sir' to him (*MC* 211). Tess uses it to Alec after his first rough attempt at intimacy: 'I don't want anybody to kiss me, sir' (*TD* 70); even after she has borne his child, she rejects his offer of marriage with 'O no, sir – no!' (*TD* 301), a response which tells much about the sad reality of one aspect of Victorian social history.

Titles, surnames and forenames form a hierarchy which Hardy conveys through choice of language. The world of *Far from the Madding Crowd* is particularly marked by subtleties of position. Bathsheba is 'Miss Everdene' to Gabriel while he works for her as a shepherd; when his emotion breaks through, the relationship is emphasised:

'Well, then, Bathsheba!' said Oak, stopping the handle
and gazing into her face with astonishment.
'Miss Everdene, you mean,' she said with dignity. (129)

Gabriel says 'sir' to his rival, the farmer Boldwood, and Liddy
the maid says 'sir' to Gabriel (203). After Boldwood's fall, Gabriel
can speak to Bathsheba by her Christian name without rebuke, and
refer to his former rival as plain 'Boldwood' (338); about to marry
Gabriel, Bathsheba speaks of him to others as 'Farmer Oak' (342).
Grace Melbury, married to the local doctor, can say 'How do you
do, Giles?' and receive the reply, 'You are going for a walk, Mrs.
Fitzpiers?' He is 'Mr. Winterbourne' to Marty, whom he calls by
her first name, but his old retainer Creedle rests on old family
acquaintance – ' "Giles" says I, though he's maister' (*W* 190, 75,
83). Poor Marian simply does not know how to speak to Tess as
a married woman. 'Tess – Mrs. Clare – the dear wife of dear he!'
(*TD* 271). The change in social freedom over the last century is felt
when Elizabeth-Jane speaks accusingly to Lucetta, 'You called my
father "Michael" as if you know him well' (*MC* 180). In the more
sophisticated company of *A Laodicean*, Somerset's hopes rise and
fall with nomenclature:

'May I call you Paula?' asked he.
There was no answer.
'May I?' he repeated.
'Yes, occasionally,' she murmured.
'Dear Paula' – may I call you that?'
'O no, not yet.'   (*AL* 146)

Later Paula speaks to him, 'Now George – you see I say
George, and not Mr. Somerset, and you may draw your own
inference'; but a letter from her begins, 'My dear Mr. Somerset'
and he reflects, 'the "George", then, to which she had so kindly
treated him in her last conversation, was not to be continued in
black and white' (274, 282). One cannot help thinking that in
some ways life was more exciting then.

Register changes are shown not only by modes of address. In
the background of informal conversation there is awareness of the
formality of polite society, and of the written code which seldom

impinges on simple life. Bob's approach to Anne Garland has an abrupt change of register as embarrassment and desire to please make him formal:

> Well, well, I won't urge 'ee today. Only let me beg of you to get over the quite wrong notion you have of me; and it shall be my whole endeavour to fetch your gracious favour'.
>
> (*TM* 158)

Formality can drop unexpectedly into the colloquial, as Angel mildly shocks his family by calling the mead 'a drop of pretty tipple' and hastily explaining that it is 'an expression they use down at Talbothays' (*TD* 167). More poignantly, the boy Jude thinks about Christminster in the terms of school reading-books and then utters his own feeling:

> 'It is a city of light,' he said to himself.
> 'The tree of knowledge grows there,' he added a few steps further on.
> 'It is a place that teachers of men spring from and go to.'
> 'It is what you may call a castle manned by scholarship and religion.'
> 'After this figure he was silent a long while, till he added:
> 'It would just suit me.' (*JO* 17)

Special registers may be assumed more consciously, reflecting the mood of the speaker. Hostile critics may suspect Hardy of a lapse into artificial diction, but there is the ring of truth in the formal language used by Eustacia and Mrs Yeobright to one another:

> 'It was a condescension in me to be Clym's wife, and not a manoeuvre, let me remind you; and therefore I will not be treated as a schemer whom it becomes necessary to bear with because she has crept into the family.'
> 'Oh!' said Mrs. Yeobright, vainly endeavouring to control her anger. 'I have never heard anything to show that my son's lineage is not as good as the Vyes – perhaps better. It is amusing to hear you talk of condescension.' (*RN* 230).

Vague recollections of the legal register spring to the lips of Mrs Rolliver, fearing detection of her late-drinking customers – 'Being a few private friends I've asked in to keep up club-walking at my own expense' she exclaims 'as glibly as a child repeating the Catechism' (*TD* 45). Henchard takes his private oath of abstention: 'before God here in this solemn place that I will avoid all strong liquors for the space of twenty-one years to come,' (*MC* 39). Military and naval registers naturally play a large part in *The Trumpet Major*. Bob the sailor finds his brother 'up to the gunnel in love', admits to Ann that after being at sea his heart is apt 'to yaw a bit, as we call it' and offers to 'convoy' her home (*TM* 203, 136). John the soldier has learned his orders of duty to his inferiors in rank:

'I am to exert over them (that's the government word) – exert over them full authority; and if any one behaves towards me with the least impropriety, or neglects my orders, he is to be confined and reported.' (*TM* 93)

His father sits more lightly to military jargon – 'only my son John's trumpeter chaps at the camp of dragoons above just above us, a-blowing Mess, or Feed, or Picket, or some other of their vagaries' (*TM* 126).

The same novel offers an example of another register which is frequent in the Victorian novel and which is difficult to place in terms of realism. There was certainly a theatrical turn to speech at times of stress and emotion, encouraged by the melodramatic style of the popular theatre. Whether this is truly reflected, or greatly exaggerated in fictional dialogue is often disputable; Dickens at times, especially in his early novels, gives his characters improbably flamboyant speech which is effective in context. Hardy amusingly shows the contrast of assumed and genuine register when Festus Derriman pleads with Mrs Loveday:

'Ask her to alter her cruel, cruel resolves towards me, on the score of my consuming passion for her. In short,' continued Festus, dropping his parlour language in his warmth, 'I'll tell thee what, Dame Loveday, I want the maid, and must have her.' (*TM* 246)

Hardy's use of stage-type language in dialogue is usually in keeping with character. It is inevitable for Eustacia to see herself as a tragic heroine:

> 'O, the cruelty of putting me into this ill-conceived world! I was capable of much; but I have been injured and blighted and crushed by things beyond my control. O how hard it is of Heaven to devise such tortures for me, who have done no harm to Heaven at all!'   (*RN* 321).

So, too, the sinister Havill is in character as a stage villain:

> 'Well, Mr. Somerset,' said Havill, 'since we first met an unexpected rivalry has arisen between us! But I dare say we shall survive the contest, as it is not one arising out of love. Ha-ha-ha!' He spoke in a level tone of forced pleasantry, and uncovered his regular white teeth.   (*AL* 140)

The individual reader as critic must decide when Hardy is being awkwardly artificial in his dialogue and when he is fulfilling the expectations of his readers. He sometimes lapses, but he was deeply sensitive to varieties of speech. His comment on a passionate outburst is significant:

> At moments there was something theatrical in the delivery of Fitzpiers's effusion; yet it would have been unexact to say that it was intrinsically theatrical. It often happens that in situations of unrestraint, where there is no thought of the eye of criticism, real feeling glides into a mode of manifestation not easily distinguishable from rodomontade.   (*W* 129)

10 Language of Hearing

Thomas Hardy's prose is the prose of a poet, and his poetry is the poetry of a story-teller. 'The Wessex novels have more poetry in them than any English novels of the nineteenth century.'[1] Hardy himself believed that good prose should have a poetic quality: 'the shortest way to good prose is by the route of good verse' (*PW* 147). He shows unusual sensitivity to sound and its translation into language. Despite some awkward lapses, both his prose and his poetry are well suited to being read aloud, a quality which is a good test of a writer's style.

It is not easy to render the auditory experience of life into words. Some of the difficulties with dialogue, particularly with dialect and deviant speech, have already been noted. Other sounds, not directly communicative, are farther still removed from the written code. Direct description is certainly possible, and the lexis of the language has developed words which convey the sense of things heard. The finer varieties of hearing are not always so readily accommodated; for example, the song of birds has a few general words, *sing*, *chirp*, *warble*, *twitter*, and some more specific, *caw*, *crow*, *cluck*, *quack*, but the differentiation of many species has to depend on a writer's ingenuity and invention. As with speech, additional devices may be needed in the form of deviant spelling, typographical variation and other ways of making the presentation more vivid. The writer tries to make the reader 'hear' a sound by building on shared agreement about the conventions which govern visual representation on a printed page.

Hardy's good ear for sound owed something to his early experience of music. His father played in the church band, recalled in the poem 'A Church Romance', and he himself as a boy played the fiddle for dances in the locality of his home; he remembered years later:

I lay in my bed and fiddled
With a dreamland viol and bow,
And the tunes flew back to my fingers
I had melodied years ago.
It was two or three in the morning
When I fancy-fiddled so
Long reels and country-dances,
And hornpipes swift and slow.   (P 648)

The pleasure of music remained with him all his life; during his early years in London he frequently went to concerts and operas. 'I am never tired of music', he wrote when he was in his sixties; 'the history of music and in a lesser degree, of musicians, attracts me always' (CL II 285, 283). Direct references to music in his work are less frequent, and less sophisticated, than those to literature and to painting. Despite his acquaintance with the formal music of the concert-hall, he writes more often of simple church music and the traditional songs of country people. The settings of his novels are not usually those in which classical music would be heard.

The musical accompaniment of church services was a memory and a pleasure which outlasted his own days of regular church-going. It has a prominent place in *Under the Greenwood Tree*, with its struggle to keep the group of musicians instead of the new organ. He had a particular affection for the morning and evening hymns of Bishop Ken, which were regularly sung in country churches, 'but is now seldom heard' he records sadly in a prefatory note to a poem telling how Hippolite Barthélémon composed the tune for the morning hymn:

And then were threads of matin music spun
In trial tones as he pursued his way.   (P 568)

When Tess asks her younger brothers and sisters to sing to her, they choose a hymn 'with words they had learnt at the Sunday-school' (TD 337).

The settings of Psalms were particularly important in country churches; both players and congregations acquired a good reper-toire. A choir has no difficulty in responding to a call for 'Psalm fifty-three to the tune of "Devizes",' (TT 14); a group of simple people respond to a memory of 'the Hundred-and-thirty-third to "Lydia",' (*RN* 67); and a family enlivens Sunday evening by singing psalms 'which, by choosing lively tunes and not thinking of the words, would be almost as good as ballads' (*TM* 131). A more sombre use of shared familiarity occurs when Henchard calls for a denunciatory psalm to be sung against Farfrae; his demand for 'Psalm the Hundred and Ninth, to the tune of "Wiltshire",' prevails over the choir-leader's attempt to substitute 'the Fourth Psalm, to Samuel Wakely's tune, as improved by me' (*MC* 206). The poems have many references to specific tunes: *New Sabbath*, *Mount Ephraim*, *Saint Stephen's*, *Old Hundredth*, *Holy Rest* and others.

Secular songs were an important element in rural life, sung to enliven the monotony of work or to pass the time on long winter evenings. Gabriel Oak's skill with the flute makes him a popular visitor at the ale-house, even though his 'mouth were scrimped up and yer eyes a-staring out like a strangled man's' (*FFM* 77). Izz Huett would help the morning milking by singing (*TD* 259); the dancing at Yeobright's house rose to a climax with 'the celebrated Devil's Dream' (*RN* 136). References to songs and dances are frequent in both novels and poems. The story 'The Fiddler of the Reels' tells of the powerful influence which a skilful musician might exert in a rural setting.

Even the more educated country characters do not evince a very advanced knowledge of music. Eustacia, a bandmaster's daughter, recalls 'the march in "Athalie"' by her moods (*RN* 82). Elfride Swancourt sings 'Should he upbraid', a setting by H. R. Bishop, 'in a pretty contralto voice' (*PBE* 53); this song is the theme also of the poem 'The Maid of Keinton Mandeville'. Emma Hardy is recalled playing simple melodies – the 'Battle of Prague', 'Roving Minstrels', 'Elfin Call' (*P* 587). In London Pierston hears a 'piano-organ strumming out a stirring march of Rossini's' (*WB* 87).

Despite his love of music, Hardy used his ingenuity much more on other man-made sounds in the life of town and country. Direct description is often employed effectively enough. Church bells are heard, recalling the particularly English tradition of change-ringing which would accompany many of the principal events of both public and private life. Church bells can be heard for a remarkable distance in a quiet countryside, and would spread news over a large area. The 'notes of distant bells, gaily starting off in a peal' announce Eustacia's wedding to Clym (*RN* 207); 'the faint sound of church-bells ringing a Christmas peal could be heard floating over upon the breeze from the direction of Longpuddle and Weatherbury parishes on the other side of the hills' (*UG* 36); Arabella knows that her parents are safely in church when, preparing for her seduction of Jude, she hears the bells 'reduced to one note, which quickened, and stopped' (*JO* 41). Hardy's close observation of things heard become movingly personal:

> And will any say when my bell of quittance is heard in the gloom.
> And a crossing breeze cuts a pause in its outrollings,
> Till they rise again, as they were a new bell's boom,
> 'He hears it not now, but used to notice such things?'
>
> (*P* 553)

Other sounds are caught by verbal description, perhaps not always so telling to the modern reader as they would have been to those who, in an environment with less background noise, would better distinguish things heard. Henchard knows that Farfrae's gig is approaching when he hears 'the sound of Light wheels whetting their felloes against the newly stoned patches of road' (*MC* 247). Sounds are different at night: 'after midnight the voice of a clock seems to lose in breadth as much as in length, and to diminish its sonorousness to a thin falsetto' (*FFM* 233). Even in a town, a listener can hear 'the familiar bang of his door, and then his quick walk towards her', as Elizabeth-Jane waits for Farfrae (*MC* 211). On a summer evening, when sounds 'extended over bush and tree to an unwonted distance', Grace hears her husband coming with 'the small remote noise of light wheels . . . . accompanied by the trot of a horse on the turnpike road' (*W* 265).

Hardy's skill with analogy, already discussed in other areas, is notable in conveying auditory experience. Description often gives way to a simile which makes its point effectively. A plaintive child 'piped . . . . like a melancholy bullfinch' (*PBE* 74); Bob Loveday, appropriately for a sailor, is heard 'occasionally heaving a breath like the wind in a ship's shrouds' (*TM* 151). There is a darker sense when Arabella, having deserted her dying husband, comes to see the college boats with 'the oars smacking with a loud kiss on the face of the stream' (*JO* 345). Sadly too, Hardy recalls waiting for his wife to return while:

Outside in the road the telegraph wire
  To the town from the darkening land
Intones to travellers like a spectral lyre
  Swept by a spectral hand.   (*P* 743)

More philosophically, a tapping a cask of brandy must refill it
with water, 'or it will cluck like forty hens when it is handled,
and show that 'tis not full' ('The Distracted Preacher').

It is with the sounds of nature, as with its sights, that Hardy
shows his finest descriptive power. Few writers have remained so
close to the countryside of their early days and evoked it so well
for those who have not known it. Virginia Woolf's appreciation
is just:

> The rain, he knows, falls differently as it falls upon roots or
> arable; he knows that the wind sounds differently as it passes
> through the branches of different trees . . . what naturalist with
> a microscope in his pocket, what scholar solicitous for the
> changing shapes of language, ever heard the cry of a small
> bird killed in the next wood by an owl, with such intensity?[2]

The wind speaks in many voices to Hardy: 'the creaking sound of
two overcrowded branches in the neighbouring wood, which were
rubbing each other into wounds' (*W* 34); 'gruffly growled the wind
on Toller downland' (*P* 250); 'winged whiffs from the north with a
husky croon' (*P* 713). The many voices of the wind are described
in a long passage in *The Return of the Native*, where the wind over
Egdon Heath 'seemed made for the scene . . . part of its tone was
quite special; what was heard there could be heard nowhere else'
(*RN* 71). Birds and animals are as familiar as human beings and
as distinctive in their voices. A cock crowing in the afternoon is
considered a bad omen (*TD* 213); a farmer passing his stables hears
'the steady grind of all the eaters . . . occasionally diversified by
the rattle of a rope or the stamp of a foot' (*FFM* 119); the
walker preoccupied with the past may miss 'the contralto note/Of
cuckoos hid on either hand' (*P* 269). The misery of Tess sleeping
in the wood is counterpointed by the sound of dying pheasants:
'sometimes it was a palpitation, sometimes a flutter; sometimes
it was a sort of gasp or gurgle' (*TD* 267).

With natural sounds too, Hardy moves from description to

analogy. The symbiosis of man and nature is emphasised: a sound is compared to one in a different realm of being. On the night before her reluctant wedding Cytherea Graye is disturbed by the wind 'sounding as if someone were beating the wall below her window with a bunch of switches' and making the trees rattle 'like a man playing castanets or shaking dice' (*DR* 263). The wind mocks Henchard on the day of his party for the town by playing 'on the tent-cords in Aeolian improvisations' (*MC* 107), and Jude in his renewed aspirations to ordination when it 'blew through the trees, and sounded in the chimney like the pedal notes of an organ' (*JO* 103). The wind often accompanies the sad life of Tess. During the hard winter at Flintcomb-Ash the roof of her cottage sounds as if it 'had turned itself into a gymnasium of all the winds'; on her fatal wedding night the dead leaves are 'stirred to irritated resurrection' and make 'noises as of silk smartly rubbed'; at Stonehenge 'the wind, playing upon the edifice, produced a booming tune, like the note of some gigantic one-stringed harp' – as if to echo the harp which Angel had played in happier times at Talbothays (*TD* 276, 215, 368). A sad mother thinks of her 'fallen' daughter when 'the tempest mouths into the flue-top a word like a curse' (*P* 904).

Water has its noises too, often menacing as befits that most ambiguous of images, life-giving and life-destroying. The ebbing sea in a storm slides down the beach 'dragging the pebbles under it with a rattle as of a beast gnawing bones' (*HE* 270), and the sea can sound 'like a hammering in a hollow tomb' (*P* 361), or 'like the slam of doors/Or hammerings on hollow floors' (*P* 494). The sea's voices change with human moods: for a young man full of hope the waves 'huzza'd like a multitude below'; in middle age he heard them 'wagging in a long ironic laughter'; as an old man he returns to the place where:

> Once, I heard the waves huzza at Lammas-tide;
> But they supplicate now – like a congregation there
> Who murmur the confession – I outside,
> Prayer denied. (*P* 427f)

The sound of water follows the tragedy of Henchard as wind does Tess: at the mill-stream in the gloomy suburbs of Casterbridge the water 'roared down a back-hatch like the voice of desolation';

conversely, the voices on fair-day sound like 'wavelets on a looping sea'; on the rainy evening when Henchard goes to consult Conjuror Fall 'ivy and laurel resounded like distant musketry'. The most remarkable passage describes the sound of the waters as they approach and reach Ten Hatches where Henchard sees his effigy in the water. We learn that 'with Henchard music was of regal power' and are then taken through the sounds of the flowing water with successive musical analogies until, at the Hatches themselves, 'there proceeded a very fugue of sounds' (*MC* 124, 148, 169, 256). Birds and animals take on human attributes in their voices. Herons make 'a great bold noise as of opening doors and shutters' (*TD* 141); thrushes crack snails on stones 'with the noisiness of little smiths at work on little anvils' (*TT* 181). Again, the analogy may go from human to animal: when Sue tears up her elegant nightdress as she returns to Phillotson, the effect is 'sounding through the house like a screech-owl' (*JO* 310) and Ethelberta, hearing of her former lover exclaims 'like a note from a storm-bird at night' (*HE* 227). At points like these Hardy seems to take us into a primitive world, older than Victorian Wessex, when links between the human and the animal were stronger and the sympathy deeper.

The representation of sounds by onomatopoeia is a regular feature of English, and of most other languages. There are words which have no apparent etymology except the attempt to echo directly the sounds of auditory experience. Many of them are conventionalised rather than directly evocative: we accept the idea that dogs say 'bow-wow' and cats 'mee-ow', that cows 'moo' and ducks 'quack'. The conventions differ between languages: French dogs say 'gnaf-gnaf' and French cocks say 'cocorico', not 'cock-a-doodle-do'. Words like *bang*, *whizz*, *tinkle* similarly are intended to give an echoic effect: here again we are brought close to something very old, perhaps even the origin of language itself. It is not easy to say whether some of these effects are really echoic or whether semantic association thus connects them. Is there anything distinctive about the vowel consonant cluster *sl-* or do we respond through meaning to a set of words like *slow*, *slimy*, *slide*, *slither*, *slip*? Sometimes the mere sight of letters on the page is enough; we probably do not 'hear' anything when we accept *ugh* as a signal of disgust and *sh* as a call for silence in written dialogue. These are interesting considerations: the effect of both conventional and imaginative onomatopoeia is without question.

Hardy uses both kinds, sometimes in a clearly literary way. He is notably fond of the word *purl* to describe the sound of water. It is an old word, popular especially in eighteenth-century poetry, which he produces so frequently as to make it a trademark of his style.[3] We read of the 'purl of waters at a weir' (*MC* 240; *HE* 139; *P* 288); of rivulets (*P* 528), of 'the alert brook' (*P* 818), a 'shallow stream' (*AL* 195) and a Cornish river (*P* 350). After the opening of confidences about his marriage in conversation with Gillingham, Phillotson is left alone where 'no sound was audible but that of the purling tributaries of the Stour' (*JO* 195). Other conventional echoic words are more familiar in daily usage: 'the old clock indoors whizzed forth twelve strokes' (*RN* 207), the curfew bell gives 'a peremptory clang' (*MC* 48), a waggon 'went on jangling over the hill' (*MC* 275).

Reduplication is a common feature of onomatopoeia: bells go *ding-dong*, and door-knockers *rat-tat*, or the 'rat-tat-tat-tat' with which Boldwood knocks on Bathsheba's door (*FFM* 83). A mill goes 'clack, clack, clack', the rain falls 'plash, plash, plash' (*P* 892, 881). A cash register goes 'ting-ting' when a coin is put in (*JO* 149), a cradle rocks with 'nick-knock, nick-knock' (*TD* 40), a butter-churn sounds with 'slip-slopping' and changes to 'flick-flack' as the liquid thickens (*TD* 131, 144). Feet go 'pit-pat', and a van 'rumble-mumble' (*P* 222, 706).

Hardy shows ingenuity in coining onomatopoeic words, particularly in differentiating the sounds of the countryside. In the early morning a sparrow begins with 'a coarse-throated chatter', then a finch 'chee-wheeze-wheeze-wheeze', a robin 'tink-tink-tink-tink-a-chink' and a squirrel 'chuck-chuck-chuck' (*FFM* 264). A fox barks 'wong, wong, wong' (*P* 734) and another squirrel says 'chut-chut-chut' (*W* 290); pheasants are heard 'cu-uck, cuck' (*FFM* 58). An unusual word, variously spelled, is the 'skirr' of a halter in the stable (*W* 236) or the 'scurr' of whetting implements (*FFM* 127).

These sonic effects are made in both prose and poetry. The fineness of Hardy's ear is apparent also in the more specific devices of verse, which is essentially built upon patterns of sound arranged according to various conventions. We are accustomed to meet it on the printed page, but the response is really to sound, with the effect enhanced by the visual pattern of lines and stanzas. Hardy thought a great deal about the techniques of verse:

Among his papers were quantities of notes on rhythm and metre: with outlines and experiments in innumerable original metres, some of which he adopted from time to time.   (*LY* 79)

He certainly used a variety of metres, though few seem to be totally original. It can fairly be said that he developed the possibilities of English in rhythm and rhyme very extensively.

Rhyme has been a feature of English poetry for many centuries, though often challenged by the dramatic and epic power of blank verse and falling out of favour with many modern poets. English does not, in fact, offer a wide variety of rhymes, and long usage in the literary tradition has made many of them seem banal and obvious. Hardy nearly always uses rhyme, except in *The Dynasts*. He can sometimes, though seldom, fall into the trap of the predictable rhyme which makes a stanza collapse into bathos:

> And what my mirror shows me in the morning
> Has more of blotch and wrinkle than of bloom;
> My eyes too, heretofore all glasses scorning,
>   Have just a touch of rheum.   (*P* 87)

> I plodded to Fairmile Hill-top, where
>   A maiden one fain would guard
> From every hazard and every care
>   Advanced on the roadside sward.   (*P* 274)

More often he is successful, usually in the full rhyme which most English poets have used; sometimes with half-rhyme:

> Do I know these, slack-shaped and wan,
> Whose substance, one time fresh and furrowless,
>   Is now a rag drawn over a skeleton,
> As in El Greco's canvases? –
>   Whose cheeks have slipped down, lips become indrawn,
> And statures shrunk to dwarfishness?   (*P* 702)

He has a particular liking for feminine rhymes, in which one or more weak syllables follow the stressed rhyme without changing the pattern of sound. The effect of repeated feminine rhymes can be to make a poem sound light or humorous, but in combination with strong masculine rhymes the sound is hauntingly evocative:

> In a ferny byway
> Near the great South-Wessex Highway,
> A homestead raised its breakfast-smoke aloft;
> The dew-damps still lay steamless, for the sun had made
>   no skyway,
> And twilight cloaked the croft.   (*P* 35)

Unrelieved feminine rhymes have a gentle, tripping sound which Hardy's gift of word selection and compounding can save from triviality:

> Fad'st thou, glow-forsaken,
> Darkness-overtaken!
>   Thy first sweetness,
>   Radiance, meetness,
> None shall re-awaken.   (*P* 61)

The rhyme may be spread over more than one word:

> Woman much missed, how you call to me, call to me.
> Saying that now you are not as you were
>   When you had changed from the one who was all to me,
> But as at first, when our day was fair.   (*P* 346)

The combination of masculine and feminine rhyme is found through the whole range of Hardy's poetry. He can also choose the plain masculine rhyme to make his effect firmly and soberly; this is characteristic of some of his best-known poems:

> Christmas Eve, and twelve of the clock.
>   'Now they are all on their knees,'
> An elder said as we sat in a flock
>   By the embers in hearthside ease.   (*P* 468)

> Only a man harrowing clods
>   In a slow silent walk
> With an old horse that stumbles and nods
>   Half asleep as they stalk.   (*P* 543)

Defying the comparative paucity of rhymes in English, Hardy attempts triple rhymes and often succeeds without banality:

> Snow-bound in woodland, a mournful word,
> Dropt now and then from the bill of a bird,
> Reached me on wind-wafts; and thus I heard,
>   Wearily waiting.   (*P* 11)

Two sets of triple rhyme compose a stanza, the repetition suggesting the weight of inevitability and resignation that pervades the whole poem:

> That with this bright believing band
>   I have no claim to be,
> That faiths by which my comrades stand
>   Seem fantasies to me,
> And mirage-mists their Shining Land,
>   Is a strange destiny.   (*P* 67)

A favourite form with Hardy is the five-lined stanza with two sets of rhymes:

> There dwells a mighty pair –
>   Slow, statuesque, intense –
>   Amid the vague Immense;
> None can their chronicle declare,
>   Nor why they be, nor whence.   (*P* 118)

Double, triple and quadruple rhyme are combined in one of the most anthologised poems, with two stanzas rhyming – ababccccb:

> This the weather the cuckoo likes,
>   And so do I:
> When showers betumble the chestnut spikes,
>   And nestlings fly;
> And the little brown nightingale sings his best.
> And they sit outside at the 'Travellers' Rest',
> And maids come forth sprig-muslin drest,
> And citizens dream of the south and west,
>   And so do I.   (*P* 563)

Even bolder repetition of rhyme is attempted, usually with a lighter, satirical effect as in the poem 'The Respectable Burgher' with its thirty-six lines all rhyming with the opening line's *declare*. A limited pattern of rhyme can have an incantatory, almost spell-like effect, and some of Hardy's poems give the feeling of the old traditional ballads, rooted in shared experience that must be transmitted to each generation. His use of refrains to link stanzas deepens this sense, as in:

> All day cheerily,
> All night eerily!

of 'Voices from things growing in a Churchyard'; 'Love lures life on' after each stanza of 'Lines to a Movement in Mozart's E-flat Symphony'; 'On whom the rain comes down' in 'An Autumn Rain-Scene'. The refrain may be within the stanza, like the delicate repetition of the name 'Lizbie Browne' or the grim 'alas for me' which ends the second line of every stanza in 'A Sunday Morning Tragedy'. The incantatory effect is given also by internal rhymes which seem to drive the sentiments of the poem on to a fate that cannot be withstood, as when soldiers' wives are lamenting:

> O it was sad enough, weak enough, mad enough –
> Light in their loving as soldiers can be –
> First to risk choosing them, leave alone losing them
> Now, in far battle, beyond the South Sea!   (*P* 88)

Alliteration is a traditional feature of English poetry, dating back to the Old English line which depended on alliterative stresses. The later dominance of metre and rhyme has never totally displaced a fondness for alliteration, which has endured into twentieth-century poetry. Hardy's use of alliteration may owe something to his regard for the Saxon heritage of English, although the more dedicated Saxonist William Barnes did not use it very extensively. Alliteration adds to the heavy, weary sense of:

> While rain, with eve in partnership,
> Descended darkly, drip, drip, drip,
> Beyond the last lone lamp I passed

Walking slowly, whispering sadly,
Two linked loiterers, wan, downcast. (*P* 315)

The repeated *d* of the second line brings the sound of steady rain; the *l* of *last* and *lone* destroys the expected brightness of *lamp*; the *w*, *s* pattern of the fourth line reinforces the semantic effect of the adverbs and the participles, and the *l*, *w*, *d* sequence of the fifth line draws all into the persons of the unknown characters. This is Hardy's sensitive ear at its best; other alliterative effects are less complex, but powerful in their context:

I lisped rough rhymes of chance, not choice (*P* 443)

What of the faith and fire within us
Men who march away (*P* 538)

Her he still holds the master mischief-mind
And marrer of the countries; quietude (*D* 2 III i)

Alliteration occasionally appears in Hardy's prose; some readers find it clumsy, others pleasing. It is often combined with the compound adjectives that he favours:

The puddles and damp *r*uts left by the *r*ecent *r*ain had a *c*old *c*orpse-eyed luminousness. (*W* 280)

When the *l*ove-*l*ed man had ceased from his *l*abours Bathsheba came and *l*ooked him in the face. (*FFM* 136)

Making it altogether a *p*leasant spot, with the usual touch of melancholy that a *p*ast-marked *p*rospect lends. (*MC* 88)

The wide variety of Hardy's poetic metres did not save him from adverse criticism of harshness and clumsiness. His contemporaries were less inclined to accept the variations of stress that became normal in the free verse of the twentieth century. A musical quality in verse is not incompatible with the occasional preference for conversational rhythm above perfect smoothness. Not all his readers agreed: *The Dynasts* came in for particularly harsh comment: 'the metrical work is halting, turgid and singularly lacking in music'; 'Mr. Hardy has a partiality for dactylic endings in his blank verse . . . the use of which betokens an ear ill-trained to the melody of verse'.[4] Modern taste is more likely to find satisfaction in the colloquial tone of:

'Man, you too, aren't you, one of those rough followers of the criminal?
All hanging hereabout to gather how he's going to bear Examination in the hall.'   (P 382)

'I will get a new string for my fiddle,
    And call to the neighbours to come,
And partners shall dance down the middle
    Until the old-pewter-wares hum:
And we'll sip the mead, cyder and rum.'   (P 465)

and not to be offended by the dactylic endings of blank verse:

And whatsoever things of gravity
It may be needful to communicate.   (D 1 VI viii)

Metrical variations within stanzas are frequent and give a visual pattern to the eye as well as compelling the attention of the ear:

I went and stood outside myself,
    Spelled the dark sky
    And ship-lights nigh,
And grumbling winds that passed thereby.   (P 499)

As newer comers crowd the fore,
    We drop behind,
We who have laboured long and sore,
    Times out of mind,
And keen as yet, must not regret
    To drop behind.   (P 146)

The metres generally assist the pervading tone of Hardy's attitude to the world, but he knows also how to use gay, tripping forms for the lighter mood:

Sweet cyder is a great thing,
   A great thing to me,
Spinning down to Weymouth town
   By Ridgway thirstily.   (*P* 474)

Stanza forms accommodate Hardy's different patterns of
rhyme and metre; he also uses some of the more traditional
and rigid forms, including sonnet, terza rima, and triolet (*P* 322,
24, 137). Some of his own experiments may seem mannered on
first encounter; they usually make their effect cumulatively as the
thought of the poems unfolds. It is necessary to persevere and not
be put off by slightly unpromising openings:

No; no;
It must not be so:
They are ways we do not go.

Still chew
The kine and moo
In the meadows we used to wander through.   (*P* 527)

The loose blank verse of *The Dynasts* is relieved by stanzaic
choruses, often in unusual classical metres:

Pushing spread they! Shout as they reach the summit! –
Strength and stir new-primed in their plump battalions:
Puffs of barbed flame blown on the lines opposing
   Higher and higher.   (*D* II iv 5)

Hardy's poetry shows a broader formal structure beyond metre
and stanza. He is particularly fond of antithesis in the whole poem,
the initial state or observation being reversed or changed by what
follows. Sequence of time and the contrast of past and present are
the factors which most often undergird the change. Too much
perhaps has been made of the 'antinomial' pattern of his work;
contrast is not peculiar to Hardy.[5] It may, however, be said that
his sense of balance and shape extends throughout the range of
poetic elements, rhyme, metre, stanza and total form. Familiar
poems like 'The Five Students', 'Afterwards', 'At Castle Boterel'
and, less gravely, 'Weathers', show the pattern. 'The Seasons of

the Year' is a short example of balanced contrast to which all the
elements of verse contribute:

> Winter is white on turf and tree,
>   And birds are fled;
> But summer songsters pipe to me,
>   And petals spread,
> For what I dreamt of secretly
>   His lips have said!
>
> O 'tis a fine May morn, they say,
>   And blooms have blown;
> But wild and wintry is my day,
>   My song-birds moan;
> For he who vowed leaves me to pay
>   Alone – alone!

11 Style and Text

In conclusion we shall look at specific pieces of Hardy's writing, to illustrate some characteristics of his language. Many features have been considered separately, with examples from different books; such analysis is valuable only as it leads towards better understanding of a novel or poem. Style is the result of many qualities which cohere in a text. Identification is the beginning of criticism but not its purpose: it is the judgements which we draw from our observations that are important. The practice of stylistics enables us to identify and describe, and then to proceed to evaluation. Its goal is enhanced pleasure through better understanding.

The judgements passed on the same text may be very variable. There is no 'correct' result of a close reading, in the way that chemistry or mathematics produce single correct answers. Personal response is a vital part of literary criticism and, provided it is rooted in the text and can point to the text for justification, no reading can be dismissed as worthless. This does not mean that the text becomes so elusive as to have no definite meaning; a creation in language exists in its own reality, but it also holds some connection with the outward reality which its readers have experienced.

No passage will show all the features of an author's language. An extract from a novel is particularly inadequate, because full criticism derives from the whole book. The culmination of linked episodes through which characters develop reveals the theme; the extended language and imagery contain the author's imaginative creation. However, a short extract treated as a sample can be a guide towards close reading of the whole.

The passage which follows comes from *The Return of the Native*. This was Hardy's sixth published novel and is widely regarded as the first of his really great books. It was published in serial form in the magazine *Belgravia* throughout 1878, in twelve parts, and concurrently in *Harper's Magazine* in the United States. A three-volume edition was published in London by Smith, Elder and Company in November 1878 and in New York by Henry Holt, in December. Hardy made some textual changes in subsequent editions.[1]

The novel is set on Egdon Heath, based on the open land between Dorchester and Wareham which Hardy knew closely all through his life; the wild, independent life of the heath itself with its flora and fauna gives more than a background to the human action and emphasises the loneliness and insignificance of people against the immensities of nature and of history. Eustacia Vye comes to live on the heath with her grandfather, a retired sailor. She is restless and unhappy, longing for romance and excitement greater than her present way of life can afford. Hardy says of her:

> To be loved to madness – such was her great desire. Love was to her the one cordial which could drive away the eating loneliness of her days. And she seemed to long for the abstraction called passionate love more than for any particular lover. (*RN* 84)

Eustacia is in love with Damon Wildeve, who is still attracted to her although he is to marry Tamsin Yeobright. On 5 November when bonfires are lit all over the heath, Eustacia gets a small boy to look after one for her, hoping that it will be a signal to Wildeve to come and see her. She has been walking on the heath, and now returns to her grandfather's house. The passage is taken from Book 1, Chapter 6 of the novel.

> Her course was in the direction of the small undying fire which had drawn the attention of the men on Rainbarrow and of Wildeve in the valley below. A faint illumination from its rays began to glow upon her face, and the fire soon revealed itself to be lit, not on the level ground, but on a salient corner or redan of earth, at the junction of two converging bank fences. Outside was a ditch, dry except immediately under the fire, where there was a large pool, bearded all round by heather and rushes. In the smooth water of the pool the fire appeared upside down.

The banks meeting behind were bare of a hedge, save such as was formed by disconnected tufts of furze, standing upon stems along the top, like impaled heads above a city wall. A white mast, fitted up with spars and other nautical tackle, could be seen rising against the dark clouds whenever the flames played brightly enough to reach it. Altogether the scene had much the appearance of a fortification upon which had been kindled a beacon fire.

Nobody was visible: but ever and anon a whitish something moved above the bank from behind, and vanished again. This was a small human hand, in the act of lifting pieces of fuel into the fire; but for all that could be seen the hand, like that which troubled Belshazzar, was there alone. Occasionally an ember rolled off the bank, and dropped with a hiss into the pool.

At one side of the pool rough steps built of clods enabled any one who wished to do so to mount the bank; which the woman did. Within was a paddock in an uncultivated state, though bearing evidence of having once been tilled; but the heath and fern had insidiously crept in, and were reasserting their old supremacy. Further ahead were dimly visible an irregular dwelling-house, garden, and outbuildings, backed by a clump of firs.

The young lady – for youth had revealed its presence in her buoyant bound up the bank – walked along the top instead of descending inside, and came to the corner where the fire was burning. One reason for the permanence of the blaze was now manifest: the fuel consisted of hard pieces of wood, cleft and sawn – the knotty boles of old thorn trees which grew in twos and threes about the hillsides. A yet unconsumed pile of these lay in the inner angle of the bank; and from this corner the upturned face of a little boy greeted her eyes. He was dilatorily throwing up a piece of wood into the fire every now and then, a business which seemed to have engaged him a considerable part of the evening, for his face was somewhat weary.

'I am glad you have come, Miss Eustacia,' he said, with a sigh of relief. 'I don't like biding by myself.'

'Nonsense. I have only been a little way for a walk. I have been gone only twenty minutes.'

'It seemed long,' murmured the sad boy. 'And you have been so many times.'

'Why, I thought you would be pleased to have a bonfire. Are you not much obliged to me for making you one?'

'Yes; but there's nobody here to play wi' me.'

'I suppose nobody has come while I've been away?'

'Nobody except your grandfather; he looked out of doors once for 'ee. I told him you were walking round upon the hill to look at the other bonfires.'

The first paragraph centres on the fire which is the focal point of the scene and the image of Eustacia's seeking passion. The words *fire, illumination, rays, glow* establish it in the reader's imagination. It is given prominence by the deictic *the* in the first sentence, leading to the particularising of the *which* clause referring to a scene earlier in the novel. Then the fire takes a stronger grammatical position as the subject of the reflexive *revealed itself*, with a description of its exact location. The fire is the subject of the final sentence of the paragraph, a short, simple sentence in which the subject is given emphasis by being delayed to the end after the leading of the adverbial phrase *in the smooth water of the pool.*

The word *redan* is a military term for a type of fortification in which two defences meet at an angle pointing away from the centre. *Salient*, originally a heraldic term, refers to an outward-pointing angle, and in the nineteenth century often to the angle of a fortification: its modern more abstract use as in 'a salient point' of an argument was also current. Hardy seems to be indulging his fondness for recondite words, applied to simple things; but the choice is apposite and will link with the thought of the next paragraph. The pool *bearded* by plants is given an epithet with human associations, typical of Hardy's feeling of the close sympathy between humanity and the inanimate world.

The first sentence of the second paragraph continues the focus on nature by making the *banks* the subject. It is a somewhat clumsy sentence with the main clause followed by the qualifying passive verb *save such as were formed*, whose agent-noun is described by a participial phrase. The closing simile, however, is startling and continues both the human and plant relationship and the sense of foreboding. The tragic judgement that will be passed in the subsequent fates of Eustacia and Wildeve throws a warning shadow through the image of harsh penal history. The *white mast* carries on the perpendicular visual image, presented through the impersonal passive *could be seen* which suggests Hardy's silent observer who is often in the background; and the sense of events unfolding without the work of the main actors in the drama is further suggested in the next sentence by the passive *had been kindled*. The military words of the previous paragraph, the mast and the closing analogy with a *fortification* all contribute to the building up of conflict in which Eustacia and Wildeve will be increasingly embattled by circumstances. The fire is reintroduced with its concomitant words *flames* and *kindled* and now takes on a warning role through its new epithet *beacon*.

The next paragraph continues both the visual effect and the sense of events developing without identifiable human agency. The blunt opening *nobody was visible* is immediately qualified by the sinister *whitish something* which is then revealed as a hand. Hardy now uses one of the Biblical allusions which are frequent in his writing. The hand *which troubled Belshazzar* was a mysterious writing on the wall at the great feast that Belshazzar, King of Babylon, gave to his court. The message was one of doom, which Daniel alone was able to interpret (*Daniel* 5). Hardy's readers, well instructed in the scriptures, would have recognised the allusion and received the hint of coming trouble. The deictic *this* which introduces the second sentence, helps to focus attention on the hand and its movement. The human element is still linked to the inanimate; the independent life of the fire is expressed in the closing sentence, short and factual, with the auditory element of the onomatopoeic *hiss*.

The impersonality and the feeling of a given situation in which the characters are only part of a greater potential, continues. Again a rather clumsy sentence opens the paragraph, making this effect through the words *anyone who wished to do so* and then bringing Eustacia back to the centre of the scene with the short clause *which the woman did*. The effect is jerky and not very pleasing, but it succeeds in showing that Eustacia, her thoughts centred on her own importance, is a very small figure on the heath, the subject only of an auxiliary verb in a relative clause. The power of the heath is further shown; we lose sight of the woman and read only of the natural setting. Hardy's liking for statements qualified by concessional structures is indulged in the second sentence. The *paddock* is made the subject, emphasised by its inversion in relation to its verb. The concessional clause beginning with *though* modifies its *uncultivated state*. Then a second main clause, linked by the conjunction *but* puts *the heath and fern* into subject prominence and gives them words of human power: *insidiously crept in . . . reasserting their old supremacy*. The human artefacts in the final sentence of the paragraph are made to seem weaker by their grammatical position after the phrase *dimly visible*. The clump of firs again affirms the power of nature, for *backed* suggests physical position but also essential support.

So when Eustacia reappears and is seen in motion, the language of the passage has foregrounded the strength of the natural world around her. The *lady* is now the unchallenged subject of the opening sentence, but her immediate movement is checked for a parenthetical glance back at an earlier one, and she does not immediately reach the main verb. It is the closing reference to the fire which leads to the next sentence. Again the woman is thrust from the centre and the connective is achieved through the semantic link between the *fire* near the end of one sentence and the *blaze* near the beginning of the next. The fire receives closer verbal description than has yet been given to Eustacia, with a detailed account of the fuel which sustains it. We do not meet her again until attention has been carried past the fire to the unburnt logs and then to another human face – the *little boy* who is now revealed as the owner of the mysterious hand. The picture is vivid and holds attention. Perhaps we do not on a first reading notice the rather learned words with which Hardy describes the rustic scene: *manifest, yet unconsumed, dilatorily*. The language which has been crisp and vigorous in describing the surroundings has become heavier. The expression *greeted her eyes* is a cliché, though its use makes it possible to give the *upturned face* the prominence of a grammatical subject. The whole last sentence of the paragraph is ponderous, with the action of throwing wood on the fire becoming *a business which seemed to have engaged him a considerable part of the evening*, rather than something he had been doing most of the evening. However, some readers may think that the heaviness of the language suggests the heaviness in the little boy with his *somewhat weary* face. This is an example of how evaluation can be subjective and individual.

The dialogue which follows brings the two actors in the

scene into prominence and asserts their humanity which the forces of nature had seemed to diminish. Hardy does not depend much on verbs of saying; the 'turns' in the conversation are quite clear between the two speakers and it is necessary only to show the phonational features of the boy's utterances: *with a sigh of relief, murmured.* Eustacia is given no such pointers, and we hear her tone as neutral, assured, as the brisk content of her replies suggests. We notice, too, the slight use of dialect which shows the status and relationship of the speakers. Eustacia speaks standard English and is regarded as a 'lady' by most of the dwellers on Egdon Heath, although as the daughter of an army bandmaster she would not have stood high in fashionable society in the wider world. The boy does not use the broad dialect which would have been his way of speech in reality: Hardy wishes only to establish his social relationship to Eustacia, not to use him as a specimen of rustic life. The dialect word *biding* and the shortened forms *wi'* and *'ee* (for the dialect *thee*) can do all that is required.

In the surroundings of her home, Eustacia speaks as one fully in command of the situation. She is formal with the boy, speaking as to an inferior, 'are you not much obliged to me'. There is a note of anxiety in the apparently casual question, made in the form of a statement, 'I suppose nobody has come while I've been away?' Her first speaking appearance in the novel gives the impression of an independent and self-assured young woman; but Hardy has surrounded her with images of conflict, judgement and doom.

A poem is generally a better text for close reading than an extract from a novel. It is an integral work, complete in itself and not contributing to a longer discourse; its share in the intertextuality which composes the poet's total achievement may be important. The poem 'To Meet, or Otherwise' was first published in the *Sphere* on 20 December 1913, just over a year after the death of Hardy's first wife. It was included in the volume *Satires of Circumstances*, 1914, with a few minor verbal changes, including the substitution of 'Otherwise' for 'Not' as the last word of the title; this is the text used here. Hardy was writing a great deal of poetry at this time, the work of his old age and poetic maturity. The poem is addressed to Florence Dugdale, whom he married in February 1914; like any good poem, its reference is not limited to the occasion of its actual composition.

TO MEET, OR OTHERWISE

Whether to sally and see thee, girl of my dreams,
    Or whether to stay
And see thee not! How vast the difference seems
    Of Yea from Nay
Just now. Yet this same sun will slant its beams
    At no far day   5
On our two mounds, and then what will the difference weigh!

Yet I will see thee, maiden dear, and make
    The most I can
Of what remains to us amid this brake   10
    Cimmerian
Through which we grope, and from whose thorns we ache,
    While still we scan
Round our frail faltering progress for some path or plan.

By briefest meeting something sure is won;   15
    It will have been:
Nor God nor Daemon can undo the done,
    Unsight the seen,
Make muted music be as unbegun,
    Though things terrene   20
Groan in their bondage till oblivion supervene.

So, to the one long-sweeping symphony
    From times remote
Till now, of human tenderness, shall we
    Supply one note,   25
Small and untraced, yet that will ever be
    Somewhere afloat
Amid the spheres, as part of sick Life's antidote.

The language is partly that of the traditional love poem, using
the familiar archaic *thee* and the words *sally* and *maiden*. The
expectation of a conventional approach is soon defeated by the
more austere and philosophical language which builds up through
the stanzas. The lovers grow to a status greater than their immediate relationship suggests and become part of the cosmic structure
of reality. The metre, too, is that of much English poetry, three

lines in each stanza being in iambic pentameter. The handling of metre and rhyme contributes a great deal to the effect of the poem and illustrates Hardy's skill in prosody and his fine ear. The iambic pentameters alternate with the less common iambic dimeter, giving epigrammatic brevity and force to balance the more discursive thought of the longer lines. Each stanza ends with an alexandrine or iambic hexameter, a line more easily accommodated in French than in English, but one which can give weight and finality when it is used in this position, as in the longer 'Spenserian' stanza. The pattern is varied by a trochaic foot at the beginning of lines 1, 14, 21 and 26 and by the unusual form of the second line with an amphibrach followed by an iamb. Further, the first line contains twelve syllables: it offers a challenge in scansion and could be stressed as two dactyls, two trochees and an iamb. Formal scansion can impose too much artificial patterning on a poem; the point is that Hardy begins with two lines which gives a feeling of metrical strangeness and fight against the conventional thought and diction which they contain.

The rhyme scheme *abababb* is typical of Hardy's fondness for repeated rhymes as the basis of his stanzas. The rhymes, which in this poem almost entirely avoid predictability and banality, hold the ideas closely together and give a strong framework to ideas which could become discursive. Hardy uses strong rhymes but does not always make them coincide with breaks in the thought and thus give the monotony of end-stopping. His use of enjambement is brilliant, creating the tension between metrical and syntactic pauses which is part of the pleasure of good verse.

The oddity of the metre at the beginning of the poem fits the oddity of the syntax. The opening words form not a true sentence but an uncompleted conjecture without a stated subject; the poet, as the speaker behind the poem, is elusive and remains concealed in the phraseology of uncertainty. The rhetorical question, punctuated as an interjection, which ends the first stanza seems to close the brackets on this mood of doubt. Yet much has been said; the capitalised words *Yea* and *Nay* are treated as nouns and seem to give the sense of dominating persons to follow the initial lack of a subject. The lovers appear only in the metonymy of *our two mounds* which presents them as dead. The personal importance of the present moment shown in the verb *seems* is drawn into the future tenses which complete the stanza, one with the distant *sun* as its subject, the other with the abstract *difference*. The uncertain, but compulsive, glide of thought from the undecided question of the moment to the certainty of future morality is aided by the undertone of *s* alliteration echoed by the voiced equivalent *z* at the end of three of the rhyming words. The sound of *s* runs through the poem, together with other alliterating sounds, a sibilant whisper of the frailty of all things.

The resolve which begins the second stanza is emphasised by the opening words *Yet I will see thee*, each of which seems to call for a strong stress and leads to the alliterating colloquialism of *make/The most I can*. The defiant *I*, now fully revealed as subject, loses its confidence as it merges with the beloved in a metaphor of darkness and confusion. The archaic word *brake* changes the tone of the statement; the proper adjective *Cimmerian*, emphasised both by its position after the noun and by occupying a whole line, is a typical but effective example of Hardy's liking for classical allusions, which his readers at the time would have shared. It refers to deep darkness, from the Greek legend of people living in a dark land at the northern edge of the world. The metaphor is upheld by words of loss and distress: *grope*, *thorns*, *ache* and the anxious seeking suggested by *scan*. The last line emphasises the condition of desolation, both semantically and by the *f* alliteration of hesitant uncertainty and the harder alliteration of *p* which seems to spit out and reject the hope of *path or plan* even as it is uttered.

The inner rhythm of the poem changes with the third stanza. The smooth, relentless progress of ideas from choice to frustration becomes more discursive with reflections on life in general. The lovers disappear into the general scheme as Hardy reflects on the reality and strength of the past and the validity of what has been done – a frequent theme in his work. The powers of *God* and the classical *Daemon* (not the modern sense of 'demon' but a kind of guardian spirit which could assume good or bad forms) are seen as equal but limited. The message that nothing can destroy the past is pressed home by both lexis and syntax. Hardy often uses negative words with the prefix *un-*, including compounds of his own making. Here the common *undo* leads to the less familiar *unsight* and then to the contrived *unbegun*. The double negation works, as it would in early English, not to create a positive, but to strengthen the negative as *nor* denies the power of *can* to do these negative actions.

The tenses of the verbs support the thought. The simple present asserts the truth of the first line, and its abiding truth in an unknown future is stated in the future perfect *It will have been*. The infinitives dependent on the present *can* are set against the completion in the past participles treated as nouns: *done, seen*. Alliteration gives additional force to lines 19 and 20. The phrase *things terrene* is typical Hardy; a commonplace, almost too prosaic word is juxtaposed with a recondite classical word *terrene*, 'earthly', and the impact is heightened by presenting the noun before its adjective. The *things terrene*, of which the lovers are a part, become the subject of the closing line, in a concessional clause which acknowledges human suffering that continues despite the defiant assertions of the previous lines. The stark reality of the Saxon words *groan* and *bondage* merges into the distant abstraction of the Romance *oblivion supervene*.

In the last stanza the lovers return to the position of grammatical subject, but only after a prolonged inversion which does not allow them to appear as *we* until the wider scope of experience has been named. The *music* of the previous stanza (line 19) is picked up in the metaphor *symphony* with its Hardyan compound epithet *long-sweeping*. The passage of long time is presented in this word and in the interpolated *From time remote/Till now*. Some readers may find the inverted and parenthetical structure of the first three lines clumsy, but if they are read aloud they have a majestic swing which overrides any semantic problem. When the word *we* at last appears, its position as a rhyming word gives a slight pause to lead into the critical *Supply one note* which is the heart of the poem's theme. Immediately the note is devalued, *small and untraced*, only to be lifted by the emphatic *yet* into immortality; the pattern of assertion and counter-assertion, withdrawal and return, is a familiar feature of Hardy's idiom.

The thought takes off into space among the classical *spheres* but is brought back to earth as the capitalised *Life* takes on identity. Again sadness is countered by hope, for life is metaphorically *sick*, but the moment of love has a share in the *antidote*, and the commonplace vague, familiar idea of sickness leads to a precise and technical remedy. The love of an elderly man will endure as a palliative in a tragic world. That is typical of what Hardy once described as 'the inherent will to enjoy, and the circumstantial will against enjoyment' (*TD* 274). Yet the word *love* is not used in the poem: *tenderness* is the nearest equivalent. Hardy avoids the conventional love-lyric which seemed to be promised by the opening phrase *girl of my dreams* and instead makes a statement about the ultimate significance of apparently insignificant human beings.

Notes

Chapter 2

1. *Household Words*, Vol. 18, 1858.

Chapter 3

1. *Saturday Review*, January 1875; *Bookman*, December 1891; *Saturday Review*, January 1899; *Saturday Review*, January 1901; *Sewanee Review*, November 1892; *The Globe*, July 1890; Lytton Strachey in *New Statesman*, December 1914; Virginia Woolf, 'The Novels of Thomas Hardy' in *The Second Common Reader*, 1932; *Nineteenth-Century Fiction*, March 1964.
   2. F. W. Maitland, *The Life and Letters of Leslie Stephen*, London, 1906, pp. 209-1.

Chapter 4

1. Estimates vary a great deal. A passive vocabulary of 150 000 words with 90 per cent of these actively available has been suggested: probably a more realistic figure is 40 000 passive and 32 000 active. See J. M. Aitchison, *Words in the Mind* (Basil Blackwell, Oxford, 1987), pp. 5f; D. Crystal, 'How Many Words?' in *English Today*, No. 12, 1987, pp. 11–14.
   2. Richard le Galienne in *The Star*, 23 December 1891.
   3. William Watson in *The Academy*, 6 February 1892.
   4. N. Page, *Thomas Hardy* (Routledge and Kegan Paul, London, 1977), p. 157.

Chapter 5

1. This point is developed in J. B. Bullen, *The Expressive Eye* (Clarendon Press, Oxford, 1986); see also J. Grundy, *Hardy and the Sister Arts* (Macmillan, London, 1979).

Chapter 6

1. In the poem 'The Impercipient' the line which appears in the revised version as 'I'd liefer not have be' was originally 'I'd rather to unbe' and at a later state 'I'd liefer have unbe'.
2. *Hamlet* II ii 555, 'That from her working all his visage wanned'. This is the Quarto reading, followed by most modern editors in preference to the Folio 'warm'd'. Hardy uses 'wan' as a verb elsewhere (*P* 723).
3. *Saturday Review*, 4 January 1879.

Chapter 7

1. R. M. V. Elliott, *Thomas Hardy's English* (Basil Blackwell, Oxford, 1984), pp. 255–7.
2. *Saturday Review*, 30 September 1871: review of *Desperate Remedies*, possibly by Horace Moule.

Chapter 8

1. *St. James's Gazette*, 2 April 1887.
2. The review appeared in the *Athenaeum*, 23 November 1878; Hardy's reply was printed in the next number, 30 November 1878.
3. A more detailed survey of Hardy's use of dialect is made by R. W. V. Elliott in *Thomas Hardy's English* (Basil Blackwell, Oxford, 1984), pp. 36–109; A valuable, but less accessible, work is V. Baugner, *A Study of the Use of Dialect in Thomas Hardy's Novels and Short Stories with special reference to Phonology and Vocabulary*, Stockholm Theses in English 7, Stockholm, 1972.
4. R. Chapman, *The Treatment of Sounds in Language and Literature* (Edward Arnold, London, 1984), pp. 67, 203, 237.

Chapter 9

1. Anthony Trollope, *Autobiography* 1882, Chapter 12: 'On Novels and the art of writing them'.
2. Review of *Jude the Obscure* in *Cosmopolis*, January 1896.

Chapter 10

1. V. da S. Pinto, *Crisis in English Poetry 1880–1940* (Hutchinson, London, 1951).

2. Virginia Woolf, 'The Novels of Thomas Hardy' in *The Second Common Reader*, 1932 (Penguin Books, Harmondsworth, 1944, pp. 187f).

3. For example, Alexander Pope, *Prologue to the Satires*, lines 149-50:

Like gentle Fanny's was my flowery theme,
A painted mistress, or a purling stream.

In English *purl* is representative only of sound, but it may be cognate with Norwegian *purla*, 'gush' or 'bubble'.

4. John Buchan in *Spectator*, 20 February 1904; *Edinburgh Review*, April 1908.

5. See particularly S. Hynes, *The Pattern of Hardy's Poetry* (Oxford University Press, London, 1961); K. Marsden, *The Poems of Thomas Hardy* (Athlone Press, London, 1969).

Chapter 11

1. A few changes, which do not affect the passage quoted, give stronger emphasis to some of the characters and their relationships.

Select Bibliography

There is a considerable amount of published work on Hardy's writings, life and background. The following list should be useful for the general reader as well as the student.

BAILEY, J. O., *The Poetry of Thomas Hardy: a Handbook and Commentary* (Chapel Hill: University of North Carolina Press, 1970).

BULLEN, J. B., *The Expressive Eye* (Oxford: Clarendon Press, 1986).

DAVIE, D., *Thomas Hardy and British Poetry* (London: Routledge and Kegan Paul, 1973).

ELLIOTT, R. W. V., *Thomas Hardy's English* (Oxford: Basil Blackwell, 1984).

GREGOR, I., *The Great Web: the Form of Hardy's Major Fiction* (London: Faber, 1974).

GRUNDY, J., *Hardy and the Sister Arts* (London: Macmillan, 1979).

KRAMER, D., *Thomas Hardy: the Forms of Tragedy* (London: Macmillan, 1975).

MILLGATE, M., *Thomas Hardy: a Biography* (London: Macmillan, 1982).

MARSDEN, K., *The Poems of Thomas Hardy: a Critical Introduction* (London: Athlone Press, 1969).

PAGE, N., *Thomas Hardy* (London: Routledge and Kegan Paul, 1977).

PINION, F. B., *Thomas Hardy: Art and Thought* (London: Macmillan, 1977).

SPRINGER, M., *Hardy's Use of Allusion* (London: Macmillan, 1983).

TAYLOR, R. H., *The Neglected Hardy* (London: Macmillan, 1982).

VIGAR, P., *The Novels of Thomas Hardy: Illusion and Reality* (London: Athlone Press, 1974).

ZIETLOW, P., *Moments of Vision: the Poetry of Thomas Hardy* (Cambridge, Mass.: Harvard University Press, 1974).

Two books of background reference on Hardy:

HURST, A., *Hardy: an Illustrated Dictionary* (London: Kaye and Ward, 1980).

PINION, F. B., *A Hardy Companion* (London: Macmillan, 1968).

Selections of critical writing on Hardy are collected in:

COX, R. G., (ed.), *Thomas Hardy: the Critical Heritage* (London: Routledge and Kegan Paul, 1970).

DRAPER, R. P., *Thomas Hardy: the Tragic Novels, a Casebook* (London: Macmillan, 1975).

GIBSON, J., and JOHNSON, T. (eds), *Thomas Hardy: Poems, a Casebook* (London: Macmillan, 1979).

GUERARD, A. J. (ed.), *Hardy, a Collection of Critical Essays* (Englewood Cliffs, N. J.: Prentice-Hall, 1963).

Books for further exploration into literary language:

CHAPMAN, R., *The Language of English Literature* (London: Edward Arnold, 1982).

FOWLER, R., *Linguistics and the Novel* (London: Methuen, 1977).

LEECH, G. N., *A Linguistic Guide to English Poetry* (London: Longman, 1969).

The system of grammar followed in this book is given a modern presentation in N. F. Blake, *Traditional English Grammar and Beyond* (London: Macmillan, 1988).

The more advanced student of Hardy's language will need to consult specific articles in books and journals:

BAYLEY, J., 'Hardy's Poetical Metonymy', *Essays and Studies*, ed. W. W. Robson, n.s. 31 (London: John Murray, 1978).

BJÖRK, L. A., 'Hardy's Reading' in *Thomas Hardy: the Writer and his Background* ed. N. Page (London: Bell and Hyman, 1980).

CHAPMAN, R., 'A True Representation: Speech in the Novels of Thomas Hardy', *Essays and Studies*, ed. B. White, n.s. 36 (London: John Murray, 1983).

EAGLETON, T., 'Thomas Hardy: Nature as Language', *Critical Quarterly* 13, 1871.

HEILMAN, R. B., 'Hardy's Mayor: Notes on Style', *Nineteenth-Century Fiction* 18, 1963–4.

HORSMAN, E. A., 'The Language of *The Dynasts*', *Durham University Journal*, n.s. 10, 1949.

INGHAM, P., 'Dialect in the Novels of Hardy and George Eliot', in *Literary English since Shakespeare*, ed. G. Watson (London: Oxford University Press, 1970).

KRAMER, D., 'Repetition of Imagery in Thomas Hardy', *Victorian Newsletter* 23, 1963.

PATERSON, J., 'The "Poetics" of *The Return of the Native*', *Modern Fiction Studies* 6, 1960.

SALTER, C. H., 'Unusual Words beginning with *un, en, out, up* and *on* in Thomas Hardy's Verse', *Victorian Poetry* 11, 1973.

SANKEY, B., 'Hardy's Prose Style', *Twentieth-Century Literature* 11, 1965.

SHERMAN, E., 'Music in Thomas Hardy's Life and Work', *Musical Quarterly* 26, 1940.

SMART, A., 'Pictorial Imagery in the Novels of Thomas Hardy', *Review of English Studies*, n.s. 12, 1961.

WERTHEIMER, D., 'Some Hardy Notes on Dorset Words and Customs', *Notes and Queries*, 1974.

ZIETLOW, P., 'Thomas Hardy and William Barnes', *Publications of the Modern Language Association of America* 74, 1969.

Index

2 Works by Hardy

(Only extended references and
quotations included.)

Fiction

3 Language Topics